"*Soon-to-be college freshmen now have a book that should be required reading for first-year survival.* Everything You Need For College *is smart, practical, and fun.*" - ***Matt Granade, former president of The Harvard Crimson***

TELL US WHAT YOU THINK AND YOU COULD
WIN $500!

We want to know what you thought about this book. Did you find it helpful? What did you like? What could have been better? To share your opinion, visit our website and complete a brief survey. We'll randomly pick one respondent to win $500! It could be you!

Take the survey at:
www.eynfc.com/survey

For complete information and sweepstakes rules, see page 172 or go online:
www.eynfc.com/survey/rules

Everything You Need For College

Publisher
Josh Schanker

Associate Publisher
Tammy O'Neil

Circulation Director
Matthew Klainer

Sales Director
Shelly Kastner

Illustrations
Sebastian Conley

Major Literary Contributors
Melissa Kendall
Patricia K. Lawrence
Alex Rubalcava
Jeremy N. Smith

Copy Editor
Vasugi Ganeshananthan

Additional Writers
Cloe Axelson
Ann Beisel
Michael Goldfarb
Mara Hitner
Carey Kulp
Jennifer Most
Robert Nathan
Scott Nathan
Eryka Peskin
Dan Sills
Jennifer Sills

TABLE OF CONTENTS

PART III: PERSONAL FINANCE 115

WELCOME!

You're no longer worried about getting in—you're worried about *fitting* in.

If you're soon to be one of the millions of students transitioning from high school to college, you can relax. Now that you've been accepted, you can forget about the standardized tests, school applications, and long, boring essays (thank goodness!) and start thinking about what you need to actually *go* to college. This is a big step, but it should also be fun, and the information in this book will get you from clueless-high-school-senior to well-prepared-college-freshman before you can say "dining hall."

You'll learn what you really need, from the ins and outs of buying a computer to the best ways to keep in touch with family and friends, smart tips for traveling to and from campus, and even how to keep your finances under control. And we've done our best to make your life even easier by including information on some of the products and vendors you'll need most, right in the pages of this book. We hope this information gets you one step closer to being prepared for life on campus.

Now, certainly this guide will be a great resource for students, but you might ask, "What about Mom and Dad?" Parents—please don't worry. Even if you don't know a CRT from a LCD, an APR from an ATM, or a PDA from a MP3, this book is for you, too. Use it to help you make informed decisions as you help your child prepare for freshman year, whether you're shipping off your first, second, or fifth child to college.

Enjoy your time before school starts in the fall, but in the words of Benjamin Franklin, "You may delay, but time will not." Start planning early for your move to campus. We are sure that with this book in hand, you'll be thoroughly prepared for the beginning of a spectacular college career.

Good luck and have fun!

PART ONE

COLLEGE
ESSENTIALS

CHAPTER ONE

OUTFITTING YOUR ROOM

Your mother will cry the first time you refer to your dorm room as "home." Comfort her: "I may move on, but wherever you are will always be my storage locker."

Dorm rooms are small, shared spaces that rarely resemble the palatial suites on "Dawson's Creek." (Your neighbors across the hall probably won't look like Dawson and Joey either.) "Thou shalt not overpack" is the first commandment of college preparation. Obey and the Dorm Room Gods will smile down upon you. Disobey, and their wrath will sock you with three extra suitcases of junk to return home during winter break.

So, how are you supposed to know what's essential for your new life on campus and what you should leave at home? This chapter will tell you everything you need to outfit your new college pad.

BEDDING

The beds in dorm rooms are longer than they are in the regular world; at most colleges, your bed will be a super-sized 80 inches long, rather than the 75 inches you slept in at home. You'll want to contact your school ahead of time to check out what size your bed will be, regular length or extra long. (Make a mental note to start lobbying for king-size water beds when you get to campus.)

If your school says you'll have an extra-long mattress, you'll need to buy bedding in this size. This includes fitted sheets, flat sheets, and a mattress pad. You should also be able to find a 96-inch blanket that will work well on the longer mattress.

There are many places to find extra-long sheets. Check out stores that specialize in college merchandise or look at some of the bigger bed and bath stores that carry a wide selection of linens. There are also various websites where you can find these specialized bedding items. And some colleges sell them directly to students.

Since space is tight in most dorm rooms, your bed will not only be the place you sleep, but also likely the place you'll lounge, study and entertain. Since it has to be such a versatile piece of furniture, choose your bedding accordingly:

- Pack two sets of sheets so you have one to use when the other is in the laundry.

- Opt for a washable bedspread in case the study break turns into a party (everything needs to be washed after a party). Prints or dark colors are good choices because they take a little longer to show dirt or pizza stains.

- Your mattress is more likely to resemble a slab of rock than a fluffy cloud. Invest in an egg crate, body pillow, or featherbed to put on top.

- A mattress pad will provide a nice barrier between you and a mattress that's slept a thousand students.

APPLIANCES & ELECTRONICS

Once bedding is out of the way, it's time to set your sights on the extras that make life comfortable on campus, starting with appliances and electronics. While your bed is your own domain, when it comes to appliances and electronics, you and your roommates should make a team effort.

Most schools supply you with roommates' names and contact information a month or two before school starts. Call and introduce yourself. Then introduce your stuff as well. Make sure your appliances and electronics are compatible: "Your DVD player or mine?" Checking with roommates helps prevent packing duplicates. A television set can be great. Four of them turn your room into a Radio Shack showcase.

You'll also want to find out what's officially allowed before toting your gadgets to school. Many colleges ban microwaves, hot plates, and toaster ovens as fire hazards, though some try to profit by renting or selling the only specially approved combination "microfridges." Abide by whatever your school tells you. Even if you don't burn down the dorm with your hot plate, you can still get burned with a fine if you get caught with a forbidden item in your room.

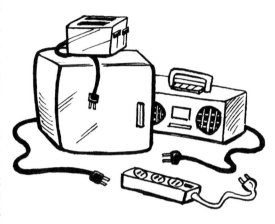

No matter what you and your roommates bring to campus, you're almost guaranteed to need more outlets than your room will have. Don't forget to pack extension cords and power strips!

Chill Out

Even if you're on a meal plan, a refrigerator makes economic sense. Your leftover pizza will last twice as long, and you can store snacks for when the dining hall closes. For those addicted to Diet Coke, buy cans by the case instead of from the vending machine. The fridge will pay for itself by the end of the month.

A small cube fridge should work for a single or double room. Triples, quads, and bigger rooms will want to get one of the larger versions. If you can find a combination microwave-refrigerator, preparing soup, tea, hot cocoa, and microwave popcorn will be easy. For any more extensive cooking, stick to one of the student kitchens most colleges offer. Whatever you make and wherever you make it, clean up after yourself, lest your school janitor quit or your roommates kick you out. A month-old cheese sandwich is a science experiment, not food.

Light Up Your Life

The quality of lighting in your room affects mood more than any other factor. Overhead lights in dorm rooms are often unpleasant or practically non-existent. You'll likely want an inexpensive plastic lamp with a flexible neck for your desk, another light source by your bed, and a floor lamp. Choose a floor lamp with a sturdy base and a dimmer, so you can switch between bright library light that encourages studying and romantic candlelight that hides your dirty laundry.

Halogen lamps produce as much heat as light, and as a result, can be very dangerous. In fact, most if not all schools have banned these historically popular lamps since a 2000 fire at Seton Hall University claimed the lives of three students. Check with your school before bringing a halogen lamp, and even then think twice about it. Another safety precaution: Never use a lamp as a coat hanger. Even if you only set off the smoke alarm, modern sprinkler heads produce 35 gallons of water per minute—more than enough to wash away your worldly possessions. You'll want to have insurance on your belongings in case something like this ever happens to you. To find out how to buy some, turn to Chapter 9, Insurance.

Talk To Me

Your phone is your link to the folks at home, far-flung friends, and the taqueria that delivers after 2 a.m. Choosing a cordless phone allows privacy as well as portability. (You can whisper sweet nothings to your girlfriend in the hallway instead of from under your roommate's bunk.) In purchasing one, look for a "PAGE" button so you can find the phone when your roommate leaves it in her sock drawer, and a "SCAN" or "CHAN" button that will search for open frequencies instead of piping you into your next-door neighbor's tearful calls to her ex. If at all possible, buy a phone you and your roommates can test and return if the reception is poor. Models vary dramatically in quality and price, and the most expensive isn't always the most functional.

A portable phone that comes with an answering machine may be a bargain for a single or double. Otherwise, opt for the campus voice mail if it's available. Resist the temptation to leave a lowbrow greeting. Professors, job interviewers, and romantic prospects will call. Don't make the first thing they hear from you, "Wassup, fools!"

You'll learn more about your options for staying in touch on campus in Chapter 4, Communication.

Sound Check

Almost everyone wants a stereo. The hard part is agreeing on the music. Whoever has the best sound system should bring it, and then rotate the DJ duties once you arrive.

Whatever your tastes, swapping MP3s and making mixes from your roommate's albums is a great way to get acquainted. Space is always limited, so you may want to trade your music racks in for CD cases before you arrive, or just record all your favorite songs on your computer as MP3s to save even more space.

Beware that not everyone likes music all the time. This especially applies to roommates cramming for finals. Although absolute silence in a dorm is a rarity, investing in a Walkman, Discman, iPod, or MP3 player will let you listen to what you want, where and when you want, and prevent roommate disputes. Though earplugs might seem anti-social, a party scene in your dorm could make them essential. At the first sight of a budding Alice Cooper on your floor, stock up.

I Want My MTV (But I Want My Diploma More)

Most student centers and many dorms boast big-screen TVs, so you don't necessarily need to pack a television to enjoy your favorite shows. Before you or your roommates bring a TV, think about whether you can pass your classes without falling prey to the soaps or taking on the time commitment to host weekly viewings of "The Simpsons" for everyone on your floor.

Likewise, bringing a VCR, DVD player, or videogame console can be a tempting, but risky, decision. There's no faster way to attract friends than converting your dorm room into a home entertainment Mecca, but you have to be strong enough to kick them out of your room when you need to study. And, you and your roommates need to be disciplined enough to avoid playing just one more game of *Grand Theft Auto* the day before a final.

FURNITURE & DECORATIONS

Organizing your room is a science. Decorating it is an art. Expect your school to supply a bed, desk, and chair, and ask ahead about bookshelves and dressers. For everything else, you're on your own. Your dorm room is your living room, dining room, bedroom, and lounge. Unleash your inner Martha Stewart to make every element work.

First, get rid of your boxes and replace them with plastic storage bins or crates you can fit under your bed or desk. A nice packing trunk can make a classy coffee table, especially if you cover it with a patterned drop cloth. All other boxes should go into storage or the recycling bin as soon as possible. They're taking up valuable real estate.

Have A Seat

If you're fortunate enough to live in a room larger than a broom closet, you'll want a comfortable couch. Unfortunately, a leather sofabed will erase your entire

four-year textbook budget. On campus, ugly second-hand couches are the rage, so anything over $150, or $50 per person, is pricey. Scout local garage sales and thrift shops for bargains. Also check around campus to see if last year's seniors left any behind. Many students find the best combination of low cost and comfort to be a futon. Futons disassemble so they are light enough to transport from store to room to storage. They're cozy enough to crash on at the end of the day, and flexible enough to extend into a bed when you have guests. No matter what you choose, buying a couch and schlepping it up three flights of stairs is a perfect way for room-mates to bond.

For those rooms with less space, individual loung-ing chairs should be on your shopping list. Cheap comfort ought to be your top priority. A great chair allows you to read and relax in comfort, but not so much that you'll fall asleep instead of study.

Inflatable seats are chic, but can be expensive. Two alterna-tives: beanbag chairs and lightweight folding chairs. If either you or your roommate is a local, maybe one of you can "borrow" a plush chair from your basement. If not, keep hunting for garage sales and second-hand shop bargains, as well as castaways from other students.

Roll In, Roll Out

Carpets complete your décor. Some floors come covered, so investigate before accepting your neighbor's prize Persian rug. If your room is bare, ask around, visit that second-hand shop, or look in the phone directory for a store that sells remnants.

Don't forget to measure before you go shopping. Merchants may be more than happy to cut a larger piece to fit the confines of your room. Thickness is a trade-off: More plush, more pleasure, but avoid any purchase too heavy for you and your roommate to carry. When in doubt about style, choose a color and design that hides dirt. If nothing fits your taste or budget, at least invest in a simple mat to wipe your shoes.

As soon as your room's carpeted, congratulations! You never have to sweep the floor.

My Walls, Myself

People will judge you by what you put on your walls. Bare walls say, "I ... am ... very ... boring." Two weeks into the term, put *something* up, even if it's the first five pages of the phone book.

Posters are far and away the most popular wall covering. Pictures of swimsuit models and puppy dogs alike will turn some people away, but your favorite athlete, singer, actor, or actress is probably somebody else's, too. Nature shots, vintage photos, famous paintings and movie stills are other popular subjects. A more individualistic approach is to line your wall with vintage record covers, foreign postcards, or a collage—be it quotes collected from your favorite authors or pictures from home, this is your chance to express yourself to passersby. Many people also find calendars or wall planners helpful to keep their studies on track.

Take care when affixing anything to your wall. Schools often have strict rules banning any changes to the room's physical structure, and they back up their threats with surprise inspections and hefty fines. Rather than live in fear or debt, choose masking tape or poster gum, not nails. Some schools will even provide these items for you to make sure you don't damage their precious plaster.

When decorating, little details can make a big difference. Curtains can give even Soviet-bloc-style housing the homey touch. Artfully-hung beads can create a meditative mood in a corner, or separate public and private space. Tapestries are affordable, portable decorations with the power to transform drab walls into the classiest element of a room. Though strobe lights and black lights are best reserved for parties, colored holiday lights can make every day festive, especially in the winter months. Anyone can put up glow-in-the-dark stars. It takes true enterprise to mount a disco ball.

Greetings

The door to your dorm room is your face to the world. Give it eyes and ears to make the most of your social life. Get an erasable white board to let visitors leave messages. Be sure yours comes with a way to attach the pen or you'll have to replace it every few days. Since using tissues wastes paper and gets disgusting when they disintegrate, pay the extra buck or two for an eraser. Though far from essential, a wireless doorbell runs about $20 in most hardware stores. What better way to cap off your home away from home? Your dormmates will wake you up the first week playing with the novelty, but at least you'll get to know them.

CLOTHING

When it comes to dressing for success, first impressions are important. As an incoming freshman you're not sure what you'll encounter on campus. Trust us: If you're worried that college will resemble a fashion show, don't be. While it's true that no one wants to run into the dream guy from psych class looking like they belong on an episode of *Fashion Emergency*, in college it's more about trying to look good with as little effort as possible. Most days, you'll be lucky to get your butt out of bed for class, so chances are that making sure your shirt is perfectly ironed won't be a top priority.

College Chic

To achieve the low-maintenance look popular on most college campuses, sticking to the basics is a safe bet. Jeans and sweatshirts are easy to match, easy to care for, and good for almost any occasion. Plus, how many times are you really going to wear those purple leather pants (at least without getting beaten up...)? So, when it comes to getting dressed without getting stressed...

Pack a few standard outfits: Go for clothes that are versatile, like jeans, T-shirts, polo shirts, khakis and button-downs. One nice sweater can hide a dozen torn T-shirts, and sweats and sweatshirts are standard wear for early classes and late-night term papers. Shorts, pants, and skirts will never raise eyebrows—unless you wear them all at the same time. Remember: In college, students don't just share a class, they share a home. If you don't spend a lot of time dressing up for the people you live with now, don't expect to in college.

Choose wash-and-wear items: Even if you're not a fashion snob, check your labels. Wrinkle-free clothes are worth their weight in laundry tokens. Consider any "special care" notice—be it hand-wash or line dry—a warning sign. You'll want to kill the to-die-for dress if you miss the party ironing it. If a shirt has to be dry-cleaned, wait until you work on Wall Street to wear it. True, a polyester blend may not be quite as pretty as silk, but caring for it is the difference between making a turkey sandwich and cooking Thanksgiving dinner.

Go overboard on underwear: As you move from the outside in, the number of clothes you need increases. Don't splurge on shoes and sweaters and skimp on socks or underwear. If worst comes to worst, you can wear one pair of jeans for a year, steal your roommate's high school gym shirt, and brush your teeth with your index finger, but you'll want new socks and underwear each and every day. An ugly rash or uncomfortable itch is the hard way to learn it's what you are inside that counts.

Keep shoes under control: Most campus closets are not generous, and shoes take up more space and weight than any other item in your luggage, so choose wisely. On most campuses, sneakers are the shoes of choice, comfy and good for walking fast when you're running late for class. Try to take no more than one or two pairs in any given color (one black, one brown), one pair of athletic shoes, a pair of dress shoes, and of course one pair of flip-flops for your trip to the shower. Before you leave, don't forget to take whatever you need for the climate (think boots or sandals).

Speaking of your trip to the shower.... Not only will slippers save you from the threat of catching athlete's foot, but they will also keep your feet casually chic in the dorm. A robe is nice when you want to walk from the shower stall to your room in more than a towel, and even if you prefer to sleep in the buff, your roommates will appreciate it if you pack pajamas. (You will too if there's ever a fire alarm.)

The Great Outdoors

When packing clothes, the first thing to consider is where you're going to school and when you'll be there. Trekking to the University of Alaska? Look for long underwear. Surfing to the University of Hawaii? Think thong.

Many students forget that they'll leave for school before summer really ends. Going to school with only sweaters and corduroys will be a real problem on those days that hit 70 degrees in September. Other students realize too late that they never thought about winter, making it a pretty chilly proposition come January when you have lots of T-shirts but no sweaters, and a windbreaker but no parka.

Half the fun of going to college is getting away once you get there. Pack what you'll need to explore the great outdoors near your campus. Then add athletic accessories like ski pants or a swimsuit. In general, it's smart to shell out the extra cash for quality clothing appropriate to your climate. Sunglasses that don't block the sun are surprisingly common, and plenty of items are only water-resistant instead of waterproof. As one wet weekend in Boston will prove, you haven't saved any money if you have to buy new shoes every time it rains.

Puttin' On The Ritz

Special occasions indoors are at least as frequent as outdoor adventures. For job interviews, formal dinners, or religious services, men should pack dress shoes and matching socks, dress pants, a dress shirt, a blazer, and a tie, while women may want a combination of some of the above, plus one or two semi-formal dresses. Tuxedos and evening gowns are rarely required at most colleges, and can always be rented or borrowed if necessary. All good roommates, dormmates, and friends will recycle formal clothes; what you wear to a fall formal your best gal pal can wear in the spring.

Students accumulate clothing:

The National Association of College Stores reports that the average student spends $300 a year on new duds.

Don't be afraid to ask an upper-classman how formal a "formal" really is. Khakis and a sports jacket are often entirely acceptable, as are a simple dress and heels. You'll probably need something nicer at least once in four years, but this is college, not Cinderella: Chances are you'll never need a top hat and tails, or a tiara and white gloves.

When accessorizing, think twice about expensive jewelry—it's far easier to steal than a 40-inch television, and far more profitable to resell than a used bike. If you're opting for the Liz Taylor look at your next formal, insure that gold watch or diamond brooch first. Don't bring anything you can't afford to lose, and that includes sentimental value. If you positively cannot leave home without these items, you can learn about insuring them in Chapter 9 of this book.

If In Doubt...

Still confused? Follow these two simple steps: One, pack only what you need. Two, take half that. If you're the first college student ever to underpack, there will be plenty of remedies: Clothing stores cluster around college campuses, catalogs and websites deliver in 24 hours, and your parents can enter the shrine that will be your old room to box and ship a forgotten treasure by the weekend. Feel free to wait until you get to school to buy climate-specific items, since that's where they'll have the most appropriate selection for the area.

OTHER ESSENTIALS

Two crannies worth cramming are your closet and bathroom.

Sort It All Out

If you learn only two life skills in college, make them balancing your checkbook and doing your laundry. After all, a college graduate who can't wash a pair of pants is pretty pathetic. If you don't already know how to do laundry, ask someone to teach you before you go to school. The most important thing to remember is to wash whites in hot water and colors in warm or cold. Don't mix the two loads, or you'll be wearing pink all freshman year.

Laundry machines at most schools require lots of quarters to operate, so keep a roll of change in your dorm room. However, a growing number of colleges also allow you to pay for your laundry with money stored on your college ID card. If this is the case, watch the balance on your ID so you can wash your lucky socks before your chem midterm.

Laundry rooms generally include drying racks or laundry lines, and there's almost always somewhere on campus that loans out irons, so luckily you won't have to pack any of those. If you're concerned, check with your school, or ask a roommate if they're packing one you can borrow.

If you just can't bear to sort your own whites and colors, several schools offer laundry services that pick up your dirty underwear and return tidy whities. These are extremely convenient, and also extremely expensive. If you're going to splurge, your best bet may be buying the biggest package and splitting it with several friends. Yes, this means revealing your push-up bras and smiley-face boxers to others, but privacy is pricey.

Don't forget to bring hangers for your clean clothes. A shoe rack that hangs on the back of your closet door saves space, keeping the floor open for sports equipment and a hamper. Hampers may be as modest as a garbage bag (not recommended) or as expansive as a wicker basket. If you can find one, the ideal is a spring-loaded fold-out bag you can pop up to load quickly, then fold under your arm when it's time to pack.

Bathroom Basics

Don't stop cleaning when you're done with your clothes. Personal hygiene isn't optional unless friends are.

First, the good news: Whatever your shower situation, you have cause to celebrate. If you're blessed with a toilet or

LAUNDRY LESSON

Getting ready for college, I envisioned a tiny room with no closet or drawer space, so I packed as few clothes as possible. I brought my favorite pairs of jeans, a few shirts and sweaters, a nice dress, and about two weeks' worth of underwear, figuring I would do laundry about that often. In general packing light is a good approach, but after arriving at my unexpectedly spacious dorm room, I soon realized that avoiding the laundry room was going to be far more important than avoiding overstuffed drawers.

This realization began at the end of my first two weeks when a lack of clean underwear signaled it was time for my first laundry load. I grabbed my detergent and ventured down to the closest laundry room, which to my dismay was located in the depths of the neighboring frat house. My route was paved with a mysterious sticky film, and a distinctly unlaundrylike odor lingered in the air. Clutching my laundry bag protectively, I averted my eyes from the open fraternity room doors, where brothers in various stages of undress watched me pass. Saying a silent prayer of thanks upon finding an available washing machine, I hastily dumped in my clothing and detergent, then returned to my dorm, making a mental note never to do laundry barefoot.

Back in my room, I was asked by some friends to go to dinner, but had to decline because I would soon have to move my laundry to the dryer. I didn't like the idea of a stranger unloading my clothes in order to use the machine. Even more disturbing was the tale of a girl who had forgotten her clothes overnight and returned to find them missing. This first laundry experience taught me that doing laundry confined me to my dorm for two hours straight, a block of time I seldom had.

As things got busier during the term, I started putting off laundry until Friday nights, only to find that parties made it even more awkward to carry loads of dirty underwear through the fraternity house. After a few months of unpleasant laundry experiences, I decided I needed to minimize the time, effort, and potential for sticky situations associated with doing my laundry. During winter break, I loaded my suitcases with as many clothes as possible, and packed an additional month's worth of underwear!

— Jennifer S., Duke University

shower en suite, the advantages are obvious. If not, appreciate shower curtains someone else has to scrub.

There's usually space to store your stuff in hall bathrooms, but don't count on room in a medicine cabinet. Bring a small bucket or bath caddy for your toiletries and cosmetics. To fill it, bring the closest approximation to what you use at home that will fit. If you're planning on leaving this in the bathroom, be prepared to share, or at least take your chances with what happens to your toothbrush when you're not looking. To play it safe, lug your stuff back and forth to the bathroom with you.

Bringing two or three big bath towels and another towel for sunbathing outdoors will keep you high and dry. For general health, pack a compact first-aid kit with headache and upset stomach medication, bandages, and antibiotic cream, as well as any prescription medication. Everyone without perfect vision will need spare eyeglasses and contacts, and a box of Ziploc bags keeps everything from toothbrushes to tuna sandwiches clean and fresh.

CHAPTER TWO

COMPUTING

If you're like most college students, you'll want your own computer. That's good, because in college in the 21st century, owning your own computer is practically as necessary as owning your own clothes. Typewriters went out of fashion around the same time as disco, and today's college students use computers for essays, e-mail, instant messaging, the Web, and MP3s.

Fortunately, although cost used to be a big factor preventing students from buying their own computers, that's not as true today. With desktop machines starting at around $500 and laptops at $1,000, computers have become much more affordable. Those of you who were planning on using the great computer labs at your college or mooching off your roommates' computers, you might want to reconsider. No one wants to realize the night before the big history paper is due that the computer lab is closed for maintenance and that the generous roommate, laptop and all, is road-tripping with friends.

With computers relatively inexpensive these days, buying new generally makes the most sense. Not only do you get an up-to-date machine, you also get the security of a warranty and avoid the possibility that somebody is trying to stick you with a used lemon. Also, any computer you buy today will likely last through your college career if you take care of it. When you think about it, the $750 you spend now isn't really that much, considering that you'll be able to get all your work done, communicate effectively, and live a hassle-free life for four years with your new computer. Heck, that comes to less than $100 a semester, probably less than you'll spend on pizza.

My own machine:

According to Student Monitor, a market research firm, 75% of all college students now own a computer.

This chapter will show you how to decide what you need in a computer, and how you'll be using it on campus.

HARDWARE

If you had entered college just six or seven years ago, this section would have been a lot different. It would have assumed you were a technophobe who thought a mouse was a rodent, RAM was a pickup truck, and the Internet was an evil force from a Keanu Reeves movie. But if you're like the average high school senior heading off to college today, you already know a lot about computers.

You probably have a computer at home or have worked on one at your high school. You've used computers to write reports, burn CD mixes, and surf the Internet more and better than most people who already have a college degree. However, since you've probably neither bought a computer

3 PIZZAS, 1/2 A TEXT BOOK, 2 LAUNDRY TRIPS, 70 GAMES OF POOL, 2 CDS, 1 LAVA LAMP, 35 CANS OF SODA, 2 TANKS OF GAS, OR 5 MOVIE TICKETS

(The Choice is Yours.)

With 10% off a TV/VCR, Surge Protector and a Printer, think of what you can do with the savings.

Hey, you don't have to be a rocket science major to figure out this deal. The RCA 13" Color TV/VCR ($249.99) is the perfect dorm room companion. But when class calls, the Notebook surge station ($29.99) backs up those last-minute term papers while the IJ-650 color inkjet printer ($79.99) makes sure they look like work worthy of an "A." Just clip out this ad and bring it in to your neighborhood RadioShack store for 10% off these three items. Simple and easy (not to mention thrifty.) Kind of like extra credit you can spend. Offer expires 6/30/02.

Bring this ad in to redeem your 10%!

#16-3304   #61-2327   #26-2389

RSS Instructions: Use the Discount key to reduce the price of any of these three products by 10%. Select Reason code "4. Promo/Coupon" and enter comment "DORM10%".

before, nor used one in a university environment, this section will provide the information and advice you need for buying a computer perfect for your college experience.

Mac Or PC

Whether you choose to buy an Apple Macintosh (generally referred to as a "Mac") or a Microsoft Windows-based personal computer (often called a "PC"), your computer should work fine in a college environment. Today Macs and PCs operate together almost effortlessly and are fully supported by most colleges. You'll of course encounter some students who are passionate about either PCs or Macs, but for those of you who think of a computer as something you use, not worship, you'll be safe choosing either platform.

PCs are the standard. They account for about 70% of computers used by college students, according to market research firm Roper College Track. Almost all mainstream consumer software works on a PC, and generally PCs come with more hard drive space and a faster processor than comparably-priced Macs.

While fewer people use Macs, the computers have an almost cultish following. As anyone who has seen a Mac advertisement knows, the machine and the software are designed to inspire. It may be surprising that a piece of translucent blue plastic can inspire so many people, but Mac fans are loyal. If you plan to use a Mac in college, rest assured you won't be alone, and you'll be able to get everything done. The majority of the work you'll do on a computer is word processing, e-mail, and Web surfing, and the Mac has the software to do those tasks at least as well as most Windows applications.

So for most students, choosing between a Mac and a PC is a matter of personal preference. However, if you're an aspiring Silicon Valley software engineer or a music-mixing successor to Moby, there are some other factors to consider. People who will study computer science should probably buy a PC, because many college programming classes are Windows-focused. If you're into graphic design, audio mixing, or filmmaking, then the special multimedia applications of the Mac make it a more attractive buy.

Desktop Or Laptop

The next big question to answer is whether your computer should be a desktop or a laptop. Strong arguments can be made for either choice, so it really depends on how you'll be using your computer.

Are you a social type who likes to study in the cafeteria? Or an antisocial sort who prefers writing papers buried in the library where nobody can find you? Do you want to use your computer to take notes in class? Will you travel a lot, perhaps because you're a varsity athlete or debater? If you answered yes to any of these questions, you should consider buying a laptop.

These days, laptops are as full-featured and powerful as desktops, so you can count on them to do everything you need. You can choose from a range of devices, from the sleek and tiny sub-notebooks that are great for traveling and easy on your back, to larger, desktop-replacement machines good for people looking to spend a little less and enjoy a gorgeous 14-inch monitor. On the other hand, if you're happy writing your papers in your dorm room, prefer taking notes the old-fashioned way (most students still do), or if you are prone to losing things, a desktop is your best choice.

Desktops are still less expensive than comparably-equipped laptops, and if you want the option of playing the latest video games with killer graphics on a large screen, you may find the low-pixel visuals of a laptop inadequate. As a desktop owner, you won't have to worry as much about your computer getting stolen—laptop theft is a significant problem on college campuses. Just be careful, because desktops do experience their own follies, like beverages

HAVE LAPTOP, WILL TRAVEL

The summer before I started college I was given a choice: laptop or desktop? I opted for a laptop and haven't been disappointed with my decision.

Just one of the reasons I've been so glad to have a laptop is travel. During my freshman year, I flew eight times. Seven of those trips involved a delayed flight for one reason or another. The cause of the delay—whether it was a torrential downpour on the Sunday after Thanksgiving or the de-icing of wings during an early snowstorm—was never especially important to me; instead I focused on the length of it. While these flight delays left many students to twiddle their thumbs and contemplate the immense amounts of work they had to do upon returning to campus, I was able to use my laptop to get work done rather than stress about it.

One example was a dreary Sunday in November just after Thanksgiving and not very long before fall exams. I had a 3,000-word paper due the next day in an English literature class and, as usual, my flight was delayed. After hearing news of the delay, I found a seat and pulled out my computer. Rather than wasting time listening to a Discman or watching TV, I listened to music on my computer and worked through the final stages of my paper. When our flight finally did arrive later that night, I was done with my paper, while other students still needed to start their work. I owed this to the convenience of having a laptop.

I now attend a school only a car ride away from home, but even though travel delays are no longer an issue, I'm still glad to have my laptop. Before going home, there's no mad rush to e-mail important documents to a home account. I simply grab my power cord and I'm on my way. In fact, I've brought my laptop on all but one of my trips, and it's proven its worth every time.

— Dan S., Dartmouth College

spilled during parties in your room. Laptop or desktop, take care of it. Remember, it needs to last you all four years.

Features

Congratulations! You've cleared the first two hurdles and you're that much closer to getting your new computer. But don't go shopping yet—you've still got a few more decisions to make.

Processor: The processor speed of a computer tells you how fast it will run (e.g. how quickly programs load, how rapidly images are rendered, etc.) and is measured in megahertz or gigahertz (1 GHz = 1000 MHz). It used to be the case that the processor speed was the main measure of the power of your computer, and that a 100 MHz machine was always better and more expensive than a 50Mhz machine. But, now there are different product lines of processors (e.g. Pentium, Celeron, etc.) that affect performance just as much as speed. A general rule of thumb is that Intel Pentiums, AMD Athlons, or Macintosh G4s are better but more expensive than Intel Celerons, AMD Durons, or Macintosh G3s sporting comparable amounts of MHz. Which processor speed and product line you choose should depend on how you will use your computer. If you are likely to use it only for word processing, e-mail, and occasional Web surfing, it's best to get a machine with a lower line and slower processor to save money. If you will likely use your machine for serious graphics, video, or music work, it will be worth it to you to buy a top-of-the-line processor. If you're not sure, choose a processor in between.

Hard disk: Your computer hard disk is like your bookshelf, movie library, filing cabinet, and CD rack in one. It's the place on your computer you'll store all those papers you write, all the video games you play, and all the MP3s you download. Most new computers should come with at least a 20-gigabyte (GB) hard disk, which is enough for most students. If you'll be editing or downloading hours of video or music, it may be worth it for you to opt for a more expensive, larger drive in the 40 GB to 80 GB range.

COMPUTER CRAZY

I'm so glad that I decided to bring my family's computer to school with me. I loved the conveniences of having my own computer, such as being able to write papers and do research from the comfort of my dorm room. However, once during finals my sophomore year my computer broke and I was forced to use the college computing center.

While my computer was in the shop I gained an even greater appreciation for computer ownership. I had heard from friends how bad using the computing center could be, and that having to use it during midterms or finals was the worst. Not unexpectedly, those days without my computer took on a nightmarish quality.

At the computing center, it was a dog-eat-dog world where it was common for students to stake out a computer and keep it for 11 hours at a stretch—even through meals and the occasional foray with friends. To lose your computer meant being shunted to the back of the long line of people waiting. In fact, it was so competitive to get a machine that people would go to extreme measures, asking friends to guard a computer for them while they went to the bathroom or grabbed a snack. In the unlucky instance that there was no one to watch your computer for you, you'd return to find your mass of papers and notes haphazardly piled on the floor next to the rest of your belongings, and someone sitting at your computer giving you a nasty look for your prolonged computer hogging.

As bad as this all sounds, the computing center wasn't entirely horrible. I admit it was very well equipped with scanners and other equipment I had no idea how to use, a beautiful color printer, ports for digital cameras, and tons of useful programs. But in the end, I was glad to return to the simple peace and quiet of my own room—and my own computer.

— Eryka P., Oberlin College

RAM: If your hard disk is your bookshelf, then RAM is your desk space. It's where your computer stores what you're working on now. Anything with 256 megabytes (MB) of RAM should be more than adequate for the average college student. Add or subtract from that again depending on your proclivity for digital music and video.

Drives: Students often use their computers to listen to music or watch movies, especially if they don't have TVs or stereos in their rooms, so it's great that almost all computers come with some sort of a CD or DVD drive as a standard feature.

If you know you'll be hosting movie screenings on your computer, a DVD player is the way to go, since DVD drives play both DVDs and CDs. However, if you don't plan to use your computer for cinematic purposes, you likely just want a CD drive, which is less expensive than a DVD drive and generally runs CDs better and faster. You may also choose to get a drive that allows you to burn your own CDs and DVDs. These are more expensive, but invaluable to students who need to transport files too large to e-mail or who have lots of data to back up. They're also great for making mix CDs for your boyfriend.

Network connection: If you're living on campus, and your computer doesn't have a connector called an Ethernet port built in, you will probably need to buy a network card. Ethernet is how your computer connects to the campus computer network and the Internet, and it's much, much faster than that limpy little 56K modem you used to dial up at home. Fortunately, most computers come with Ethernet built in, so you shouldn't have to buy anything extra. If

you're living off campus and you plan to use your computer with a cable or DSL modem, you will also need an
Ethernet port or network card.

Modem: You probably won't use a modem much at college
because of your lightning-fast Ethernet connection, but if
you live off campus, have a laptop, or plan to use your computer at home during breaks, you should also get a built-in
56K modem for dial-up access to the Internet when you're
off the campus network.

Wireless: Some more techno-friendly schools have built
infrastructure for wireless access to the Internet and university network from anywhere on campus. If your school has
this, you may want to purchase a wireless card (costing
about $100) or buy a computer with wireless capabilities
built in (increasingly common in newer, high-end laptops).
Having a wireless card will allow you to research your paper
and sunbathe in the freshman quad at the same time, not to
mention let you to check your e-mail during a boring lecture.

Ports and connections: Today just about anything you'll
plug into your computer can go into a USB port, and almost
all computers you buy will have at least one. Just make sure
any peripherals you own (like a printer or digital camera)
are compatible with the ports on your computer.

SOFTWARE & PERIPHERALS

The same way the perfect hat, handbag, or shoes complete
an outfit, software and peripherals complete your computer
system. The software you use will transform your computer
into an indispensable tool for studying, communicating,
and entertaining. Your peripherals, the pieces of hardware
that aren't part of the computer itself but attach to it, will
allow you to customize your computer depending on what
you use it for: For example, a printer if you're a big writer, a
Personal Digital Assistant (PDA) if you're a busy bee, or a
digital camera for either fun or lab work. Read on and think
about how you'll want to use your computer once you get it.

Software

Most students spend the majority of their time using a small number of applications that come preloaded at purchase, are free for downloading over the Internet, or are offered at substantial discounts for students from campus technology stores. As a student you'll need software for:

Office productivity: Here the dominant standard is Microsoft Office, which comes preloaded with many PCs running Windows. You'll use its suite of programs for many tasks: Word for writing papers, Excel for calculating data in statistics class, PowerPoint for presentations, and Outlook or Outlook Express for e-mail, calendaring, and contact management. If you think of Microsoft as the Evil Empire, you can check out Lotus SmartSuite, Corel WordPerfect Office, or Sun's Star Office, although consider yourself forewarned—almost nobody uses them, which makes having someone proof your history essay more difficult. Mac users can also get Office preloaded, or try Appleworks as an alternative.

Web browsing: You'll use a Web browser every day for accessing the Internet. Microsoft Internet Explorer is the standard, with Netscape and Opera being good, well-supported alternatives. At least one browser should come preloaded on your new computer. The others are available for free download at their company websites.

Instant messaging: Instant messaging may already be second nature to you, as teenagers are among the heaviest users of this technology that allows you to type a message to a friend and have it pop up instantly on their computer screen. AOL Instant Messenger is the most popular service, with Yahoo! Messenger, MSN Messenger, and ICQ as alternatives. Unfortunately, while all are free for download at their company websites, none of them work with each other, so choose the one most commonly used at your college or by your high school friends at other colleges.

E-mail: Your college will give you an e-mail address; how you choose to access it is a matter of preference and availability. Most students use Microsoft Outlook or Eudora Light (free for download at the company website). Many schools also let you access your e-mail using some version of Telnet (you'll find out what this is when you get to school), or a Web interface, meaning you can check your e-mail wherever you can find a Web browser. Unless you buy Microsoft Office and get Outlook included, there's no compelling reason to pay for software. For more information on using e-mail at college, please see Chapter 4, Communication.

MP3s: With MP3s, you no longer have to bother lugging your heavy CD collection around—just record your music on your computer. Most college students use Microsoft Media Player (built into all Windows machines), Winamp, or MusicMatch Jukebox, all available for free online. Apple includes the popular iTunes MP3 software on every computer it sells.

Printers

The great Do-I-Get-A-Printer-For-My-Room Debate continues to rage among students, with no clear answer. It may not be necessary if you attend a university with good computer facilities. Then, you may be able to configure your computer to print to any printer on campus, allowing you to pick up your paper as you rush to class. In addition, an increasing number of professors request that work be submitted via e-mail instead of on paper.

That said, you may prefer the security of having a printer in your room, where you can be sure that someone else won't be printing out four copies of a 90-page thesis ahead of your little three-page assignment. If you do decide to buy a printer for your room, you have two standard choices:

Inkjet: If you think you'll be printing only a handful of papers per semester, or if you value the ability to print in color, then you should purchase an inkjet printer. Inkjets are cheap and reliable, often costing under $200. Most inkjets can print a five- to 10-page paper in about a minute. Although inkjet makers like to advertise the high resolution of their printers, any improvement above 720 dots per inch (dpi) will be imperceptible to the human eye (at least for black text). If you are going to be doing more heavy-duty

printing, and you're worried about spending $30 on ink cartridges every few months (inkjets eat through ink like frat boys through pretzels), then you should consider spending the extra money for a laser printer.

Laser: A good laser printer will likely set you back more than $300, but since they are pretty durable, you may also be able to buy a used one more cheaply, either from someone you know or over the Internet. You should only consider a laser printer if you're going to be doing heavy-duty writing and need fast, cheap printing—if you're an English or history major or the next Edgar Allen Poe. Color laser printers usually cost more than $1,000, so even a graphic artist who needs high-end printing will likely use the school's facilities and get an inkjet for regular use.

Monitors

If your computer doesn't have a monitor attached—most likely if you have a laptop or one of the desktops like the Apple iMac—then you have a choice between a traditional

CRT monitor and a newer, smaller, flat-screen LCD. Here's how you should choose:

CRT: Short for cathode ray tube, these monitors look like televisions and weigh almost as much. They are cheap and reliable; for a few hundred dollars you should be able to get one in the 17- to 19-inch size range, which is more than adequate unless you plan to do heavy video or graphics work. Monitor quality is measured in dot pitch, with decent monitors between .22 and .27. Lower dot pitch is better, but more expensive. If you're buying in person, spend a few minutes staring at monitors to choose one with which you're comfortable. Inferior monitors can strain your eyes, and no professor has ever given an extension for that.

LCD: Short for liquid crystal display, these are like free-standing laptop monitors. They are smaller than CRTs, and high quality, but also generally expensive. They make the most sense for college students for whom a high price is less important than a lack of dorm and summer storage space. LCD prices drop considerably every few months, so check prices to see if it makes sense for you.

PDAs

No, this kind of PDA is not the Public Display of Affection that got you and your girlfriend in trouble at summer camp. In this case, PDA stands for Personal Digital Assistant, a type of pocket computer you use to keep track of your assignments, classes, labs, and contacts. PDAs can be pricey, but many college students find them vital for everything from keeping track of extracurriculars to checking scores of athletic events.

The most popular PDAs at college are those built on the Palm and Windows CE platforms. Palm devices are generally cheaper than their Windows CE counterparts, but other than that, what you should buy is largely a matter of personal preference.

Digital Cameras

While it's not time to throw out your old film cameras yet, digital cameras are becoming very popular as they get cheaper and easier to use. Many college students use digital cameras to avoid film and processing costs, and because they can e-mail their friends free duplicates of their spring break photos. On a more academic note, many students planning to take biology or other lab courses might find digital cameras useful in monitoring experiments. How better to remember what that partially-dissected frog looked like than to take a picture?

Surge Protector

In many colleges, dorms were built back when students wore ties to class. As such, they have brittle electrical systems, which make a $20 surge protector a very good investment. You don't want a power spike to destroy that new computer. Besides, most dorm rooms aren't equipped for plugging in more than a lamp, so you'll need a power strip just for the extra outlets.

SHOPPING FOR YOUR SYSTEM

Whew! So now that you know what you're looking for, you just need to know where to shop for the darn thing so that you can get it already. When shopping for your computer, you have a number of different options:

Ordering Online

Generally if you know exactly what you want, ordering online (in many cases direct from the manufacturer) is usually the best way to purchase a computer. It is the easiest way to shop around for the best price, and many manufacturers give you the option of customizing your computer. When comparing the cost of buying online, be sure to include shipping costs in the totals. It might seem like you're getting a good price, but you wouldn't be the first person fooled by a sneaky retailer who makes up for a low price on the computer by charging you an arm and a leg for shipping.

Buying From A Traditional Retailer

If you are the tactile type who wants to play around with a demo computer before buy-ing, or want assistance in choosing between models, buying through a traditional retailer is a good way to pur-chase your computer. Having someone guide you through a store's wide selection of com-puters can be very helpful—although beware of salespeo-ple who aren't knowledgeable or who try to pressure you into a quick purchase. In addi-tion, if something goes wrong with your computer, you can  always bring it back to the store, a feat more difficult when you've purchased it online.

Purchasing Through Campus Stores

There are advantages to buying your computer before mov-ing to campus, since you'll have time to set it up and get familiar with it before classes start. However, if you're mov-ing across the country to go to school and don't want to worry about shipping your computer, it might be smarter to purchase one when you arrive. If you decide to wait until you arrive on campus to buy your computer, you should check out the campus store. While they're likely to have a smaller selection than most retailers, campus stores often offer special student discounts. Another bonus: Anything you buy on campus will be familiar to your college's technicians, so if your machine is ever infected by a virus or just plain unwilling to start, you can get help more easily.

Warranties

No matter how you buy your computer, you will likely be encouraged to buy an extended warranty package or something along those lines. These are supposed to protect you in case your computer breaks on the day after your warranty expires, which is in fact the second most popular day for computers to break, right behind the day before your biggest term paper is due. Since most people never use these warranties, they represent almost pure profit for the retailer, and they are typically not a great deal for the consumer.

If you are very scared about the health of your computer, and are meticulously organized such that you can hold onto the warranty certificate for three or four years, and know exactly where to find it in the midst of a computer meltdown crisis, then this kind of extended protection plan could make sense for you. Just about everyone else will probably be better off buying a computer with a good basic warranty, relying on the school's computer help service, and hoping for the best.

Rebates

Yet another thing to watch for when buying a computer: rebates. These days, lots of stores lure you in by advertising prices that include significant mail-in rebates. These rebates may come straight from the manufacturer and only require you to fill out a postcard or two—or they may be tied to you signing up for additional services, like expensive Internet access for the rest of your natural life. So before you believe the prices you see in Sunday's paper or in that Internet ad, make sure you read the fine print.

CHAPTER THREE

BOOKS & SUPPLIES

Books. You remember books, don't you? They're those little pieces of paper glued together with words on the inside. W-o-r-d-s. Good. You remember.

College classes require reading and lots of it. That's a good thing—nothing makes you smarter faster than books. But nothing puts a bigger dent in your budget at the beginning of each term, either. This chapter will tell you all you need to know before heading to the bookstore.

Buy Or Borrow?

Books cost only a fraction of what tuition does, but at upwards of $500 a year, they may be your next biggest expense. Save as much money as you can by getting some of your reading from the library. At the same time, keep in mind that no one can borrow everything they need to read. Without full-time access to some books, your grades will slump and so will your IQ.

There will be exceptions to every rule, but consider buying a book if it is a classic to keep for a lifetime (*Moby Dick*), a seminal text in your field (Kernighan & Ritchie's *The C Programming Language*), something you'll need to read often or over an extended period (*The Elements of Style*), or a work you ought to take notes on (*An Introduction to Modern Astrophysics*).

On the other hand, consider borrowing if the book is a reference you only need for one week, you're only reading one essay in an anthology, or you already know the material but want a quick refresher.

New Or Used?

So you've decided you need your own copy of a book, but how do you know whether you should buy it new or used? There are some books that you simply can't get used, including new works, new editions, or textual updates (think scientific works), and others that you don't want to buy used, such as important reference and introductory texts that you plan to keep because they're relevant to your specialty. For all other books, consider saving money by buying used.

Although you might think it's hard to start your new life with somebody else's castaways, there are a surprising number of used books on the market that look like they've never been opened. (Imagine that!) When shopping for used books, flip through the pages first to make sure they're intact, and keep an eye out for excessive highlighting or numerous notes in the margins that will distract you. (On the other hand, these notes may help you too.)

Remember that whether you buy new or used, you can usually make some dough by selling books back to the campus store, although for very reduced prices. Oh, well—for all those books you'll never open again, you won't want to store, move, or ship them during the summer anyway.

Old Reliables

Having a few high-quality references in addition to assigned texts will help increase your term paper grades. Your computer may come with a dictionary or thesaurus as part of its software package, or you may use one of the many reference websites available online, but sometimes your own copy of a trusted reference text is more reliable. You'll be glad if you add the following to your bookshelf:

Dictionary: Look for a college edition with a large editorial team like the *American Heritage Dictionary.*

Thesaurus: You'll need it to investigate simple synonyms or antonyms, but using a thesaurus alone to find a word's meaning is idiotic, imprudent, and ill-advised. Try one from Roget's.

Book of quotations: Wax eloquent in every paper with a collection of quotations; Bartlett's is the old standby.

Book on grammar and usage: Write well rather than good with a grammar guide such as Strunk & White's *The Elements of Style* or Fowler's comprehensive *Modern English Usage.*

BOOK SMARTS

As a freshman, I enrolled in Chemistry 101, a large lecture course with over 200 students. After our first class, I walked straight to the campus bookstore to buy my textbooks, but as I went down the aisles referring to the list of required books for chemistry, my heart raced as I reached the section for my course—the shelf was empty.

The bookstore was very busy, so I figured they just didn't have time to restock the shelves. I couldn't be more wrong. The manager told me they were sold out of Chemistry 101 textbooks, and they weren't planning on ordering more. This was ludicrous! How could they not order enough books for everyone in the class? The manager explained that they only order enough books for 80% of the class, figuring that many students will either drop the class or use the books on reserve in the library. He added that I could place an individual order for the books, but it would take three weeks for the shipment to arrive.

At this point, I was annoyed, but thought I could deal with the library for three weeks. However, I soon learned that the library only had two books on reserve for the remaining 40 students without texts. There just wasn't enough time for everyone to share the books—I had to take matters into my own hands.

I went on the Internet to see if I could order my missing textbooks. I was surprised at how easy it was to locate the exact texts and editions that I needed. I could buy them new or used, and many of the books were selling for 10-30% below the bookstore prices. Plus, if I paid a little extra, I could get the books delivered overnight, instead of waiting the three weeks for the bookstore!

I was beyond relieved when I got my books the next day. I was able to start my reading and keep on top of my assignments, unlike many of the students who took their chances at the library.

— Michael G., Brandeis University

Guides for research papers: Ask your professors what format they prefer for research papers. The top two choices are the Modern Language Association and the Chicago Manual of Style methods, but your school may have its own system.

Foreign language dictionary: If your school has a language requirement or you're planning to study abroad, don't forget your foreign language dictionary. If you have one from high school, bring it along. If you need something more than that, your professors will tell you once you get there.

Where To Buy

When shopping for books, timing is everything. If you're considering buying used books, shop early to make sure clean, readable editions are still in stock. If you're shopping for new books, time is a little less of the essence—just make sure you get there before your books are sold out and you're 200 pages behind in reading. Whatever you're shopping for, here's where to look:

Campus bookstores: Most students head here to purchase books because it's close by and carries all the texts for classes in session. The drawback is that campus bookstores might not always offer the best prices, since they often don't have a lot of competition. However, they are probably your best option for selling books back at the end of the term.

Shopping online: Modern technology means all books in print—and some books out of print—are available online. Some sites offer used books, some offer new works at discount prices, and some do both. Other sites connect you with people looking to sell their used texts or simply exist to help you look up prices on books for sale. Comparing prices online gives you a better chance of landing a bargain. But for every time shopping online saves you a buck, there's a time that it could cost you more. Before you click

"submit," make sure you've done your research. For general literature, online discounts may be no better than those offered at your local bookstore, and returns are difficult if not impossible. Furthermore, make sure your savings justify the shipping and handling fee and that your order will arrive before midterm grades. Shopping online could be your only choice if your campus bookstore sells out of a text you need. Often, class enrollment is higher than expected. But even if the college adds a section to the schedule, it doesn't mean the bookstore adds more books to its order.

Bring It (From Home)

By all means, bring your favorite books from home, and any you think might come up again in class. Think reading *The Scarlet Letter* a second time is tough? Try buying it twice.

Don't pack books from home if you're running short on space; mail them instead. The post office offers a steep discount to send texts "book rate." It may take an extra week or two for your books to arrive, but the savings are substantial.

Two books you should consider bringing with you to college are your high school yearbook and family photo album. Everybody will want to know how dorky your debate partner really was before you gave her a makeover and what Uncle Albert looks like in his pink tuxedo.

Lock, Stock, And Supplies

Although your books may be a little heavier and come with fewer pictures than they used to, shopping for school supplies in college is little different from what it was in third grade. To write, you'll need notebooks, folders, pens, pencils, a sharpener, printer paper, and Wite-Out. You'll need a ruler and a calculator with fresh batteries to keep your numbers exact. You'll also want scissors, Scotch tape, a stapler, staples, and paper clips. A see-through plastic desk organizer keeps your supplies in order, and shows when you're running low.

A small sliding drawer and hanging file folders can be the ultimate desk space saver. An accordion file is another way to keep your bank statements separate from your magazine subscriptions, and your English assignment apart from your first-year orientation photos.

In addition to your school supplies, before you leave home, fill an address book with everyone's contact information (leave space for new phone numbers and e-mail addresses for when other college-bound friends get them), and then buy envelopes and stamps to keep in touch when e-mail isn't enough. Getting mail all your own is one of the simple pleasures of college.

COMMUNICATION

When you move to college, keeping in touch with friends and family from home won't be as easy as it used to be. After all, you won't just be down the hall or across town anymore. But you don't want to miss out on what's going on at home, how the old football team is doing, or how your little sister likes junior high, either. In this chapter, you'll read about your options for staying in touch.

TRADITIONAL PHONE SERVICE

If you're going to school far from home, or have friends on distant campuses, you'll have a variety of options for keeping in touch with them: long-distance service, phone cards, toll-free numbers, collect calls, and dial-around numbers.

Close To Home

If you're lucky, your college will give you basic local tele-phone service in your dorm room, either through a phone jack or by actually giving you an old-fashioned desk phone to use. This allows you to make local calls at no charge.

If you're even luckier, your phone system might come with a bunch of bells and whistles, like three-way calling, voice mail, and call-waiting, either at no charge or for a small fee. Each college has its own setup, of course, so find out what the situation is before you get there. It may affect what kind of phone you buy, or if you purchase an answering machine.

To place a call, you'll often have to dial a number (usually 9) to get an outside line, but when calling someone on cam-pus, you can just dial their extension. Because of this arrangement, you should know that depending on your col-lege, 911 might not be the emergency number! This is important—if your roommate decides to burn that midterm she flunked and accidentally catches her hair on fire, inad-vertently dialing the library is probably not going to help.

Those whose dorms do not come equipped with local phone service and those living off campus need to set up their own service. In many areas, only one phone company serves the whole region. In other areas, you may choose between competing companies. Regardless of the company you are dealing with, there are usually a few different kinds of plans to choose from.

The lowest monthly fee plan is usually best for people who won't use the phone a lot, since they typically charge more for each call you make. However, this may be your best option if you'll be making most of your calls through your cell phone. On the other hand, an unlimited local plan may seem more expensive, but doesn't cost as much per call, so it's best for those who will make a lot of local calls. Yet another option is a regional plan that covers not just calls in your local area, but also those across state or to neighboring states. If you're in Dallas, and your significant other is in Austin, for example, a regional plan might be what you need. Think about who and how often you'll be calling, and choose your plan accordingly.

Far And Away

When living in a dorm, you may not have a choice in long-distance providers, but this should not severely limit your options. Although many colleges sign contracts with one particular company to provide all campus long-distance service, there are still ways to make the phone calls you want and pay what you can afford, by using things like

 phone cards and special numbers, or by using a cell phone.

Depending on the college's plan and your calling habits, this one-size-fits-all approach can either be convenient or a hassle, cheap or expensive. If your college has only one provider, learn about its plan and then either sign up for this service or opt to use a combination of the local service you have in your room and toll-free numbers, dial-around numbers, or phone cards to make your long-distance calls. You will learn more about these options later in this chapter.

If you decide to sign up with your college's plan, depending on your school's phone system, you may be required to put in a personal access code before each call. This may seem annoying at first, but schools do it to make sure that if you're paying the bill, you're the person who's making the calls. You'll have your code memorized soon enough and you'll be thankful that your roommate can't rack up charges calling her psychic friend on your bill.

If your college does not lock you in to one long-distance provider, or if you're going to live off campus, the best way to find the long-distance plan that's right for you is to check company websites for more information. In evaluating long-distance plans:

Look for the best rates at the times you're most likely to call: Choosing a plan that offers 5 cents a minute may sound great, but if it's only for nights and weekends, and you make all your calls during the weekdays when it costs five times as much, it won't be such a bargain.

Take a close look at monthly fees: A lot of plans have monthly fees, and others have minimum monthly use thresholds. If you're not going to be making many long-distance calls, there's little need to pay a monthly fee to get a lower per-minute rate.

Get something for nothing: You're a valuable customer. Take advantage of the competition for your business when signing up for your long-distance service, and you might end up with something for free, like calling time, prepaid calling cards, or frequent flyer miles.

Whether you think signing up for long-distance is right for you or not, you should still take the time to learn about your other options for calling. Collect calls, dial-around numbers, phone cards, and cell phones can all be used in conjunction with or instead of long-distance service.

Dial-A-Discount

In almost all cases, as long as you have local service in your room, you can still place long-distance calls by calling collect (or by using a calling card, which you'll learn more about later). If you're paying for your own local service (you're not getting it for free from the college), you'll also be able to make long-distance calls by using dial-around numbers (10-10, 10-20, etc).

Collect calls: One way of calling long distance is to make a collect call from your dorm room or a pay phone. With collect calls you either ask the operator or use a toll-free access number (such as 1-800-COLLECT or 1-800-CALL-ATT) to place a call that is billed to the number you dial, or in some cases, to a third-party number that you specify.

Long-Distance Competition

According to smartprice.com, a consumer information website, there are over 1,200 long-distance service providers in the US.

Personal 800 numbers: This is another popular way for families with kids in college to make sure they phone home. Essentially, having a personal 800 number is like assigning a toll-free number to your parents' phone at home, so you can call using any phone and the charge will be billed to your parents. Many families find a personal 800 number very convenient, but rates can be higher than normal long-distance. Check with your parents' phone company to find out if this is a service it offers.

Dial-around numbers: Dial-around numbers bypass your regular long-distance provider in favor of a third party that offers a better rate. Because charges are billed to the person who originates the call, not the recipient, dial-around numbers can only be used from phones for which you already pay for local service. If you live off campus or pay for your local phone service, consider using these numbers to save on your long-distance bill. However, exercise caution—make sure you won't be charged a monthly fee, and be careful to understand the rates. It may cost just 99 cents to make a 20 minute call, but it costs the same to leave a 30-second voice mail message.

Phone Calling Cards

If you don't sign up for long distance, or even if you do, phone calling cards provide another long-distance option. In general, there are three types of phone cards you can use to call from anywhere, to anywhere:

Traditional cards: Traditional calling cards are often issued in connection with a residential long-distance plan, such as your parents' plan at home. All calls you make using the card will be billed monthly to your parents' phone bill. These cards offer flexibility, since you can call anyone from anywhere, but they can get fairly expensive. If you don't want to be disowned when your parents get a very large phone bill, pay attention to what you are paying per minute, and how much you are calling.

Prepaid cards: Prepaid calling cards work similarly to traditional calling cards, but as the name suggests, you pay a certain amount of money in advance for all your calls. These cards also offer flexibility and convenience because you can use them anywhere and buy them in a wide variety of places—from drug stores to gas stations. Plus, if you're a heavy phone user, using a prepaid card can help you manage your budget because you can only spend as much as you paid for the card. However, there is the risk of losing the card along with all the money you have on it. You should also beware of cards with extra charges, such as connection fees, or surcharges that apply at pay phones.

Credit cards: Finally, you can sometimes use your credit card to pay for long-distance calls, either by signing up with a company offering phone cards that are billed to your credit card, or by using a credit card directly to charge a call.

CELL PHONES

It is not surprising that according to a survey taken by research company Student Monitor, cell phones are the in-thing on campus. One in five freshmen gets a cell phone before starting college, and over 50% of all college students have one.

Just few of the many reasons students get a cell phone include:

- Cell phones are convenient for connecting with someone, anytime, anywhere.

- Cell phones offer additional safety when walking home alone, driving to and from campus, or in case of an emergency.

- Cell phones allow you to keep one phone number—no more changing numbers every time you move. (Currently you have to change numbers if you switch carriers, but there are governement regulations being developed that should allow you in the future to keep your number even if you change cell phone providers.)

- Cell phones mean no sharing a phone with roommates or missing important messages.

On top of all these benefits, cell phones are also getting cheaper to use—to the point of being competitive with traditional phones, even for long-distance. As a result, many students are actually ditching their traditional phones and using their cell phones exclusively!

Calling Plans

When deciding to get a cell phone, the first thing to do is to shop for a plan. Before thinking about where you're going to use the phone and what features you want, you should figure out whether a traditional monthly plan or a prepaid plan works better for you.

Traditional monthly plans: These plans are the most common. Your service provider charges you a set monthly fee in exchange for a certain number of minutes, usually some combination of "peak" and "off-peak" minutes (although some companies also use so-called "anytime" minutes), and a group of features, like free long-distance, call-waiting and voice mail. Traditional plans can be a good choice because:

- They are less expensive on a per-minute basis. Usually, a minute of talk time on a monthly plan will cost half as much as one on a prepaid plan.

- They often include long-distance, or offer favorable rates on long-distance compared to prepaid plans.

- You have more flexibility in which features you use on your phone, like wireless Web or roaming into analog areas, that you might not get with prepaid service.

- They are convenient; you use what you need and pay at the end of the month.

Prepaid plans: As with prepaid phone cards, with these plans you pay for your minutes and services before you use them. Some of the advantages of choosing prepaid service include:

- You can use prepaid minutes over a two- or three-month period, so you don't lose your minutes if you don't use them in any given month.

- They don't require a credit check; bad credit or no credit is not a problem.

- There are no monthly service fees or bills to pay.

- It's easier to budget; you decide much you will spend and don't have to pay for monthly airtime you don't use.

- There's no contract to sign or cancellation fees to pay if you change your mind.

As a rule of thumb, anyone with bad credit or no credit may need to get a prepaid plan unless they consider getting service in their parents' names. You may also need to do this if you are a minor (under 18). Otherwise, if a cell phone service provider lets you sign up for a monthly plan, even though you have poor credit, they will probably require a hefty up-front deposit to do so.

Anyone else can choose between monthly and prepaid plans. Prepaid plans are probably more appropriate for anyone who won't use their phone very much. Traditional plans may be good for those who plan on using their phones a lot, those who want to make a lot of long-distance calls, or anyone who wants to take advantage of all the extra features more likely to be available with a monthly plan.

Once you've decided if you're looking for a monthly or prepaid plan, it's time to think about how you are going to be using your phone and what features you want. When deciding between plans, ask yourself:

Where Am I Going To Use My Phone?

When it comes to coverage, there are basically three types: local, regional, and national.

If you go to school near home and don't plan to stray too far outside the area, a local plan that offers cheap, basic coverage may be something you want to consider. These plans tend to focus on a metropolitan area or one state, but will charge extra for any calls made outside that area. One step up from the local plan is the regional plan, which

Huge New World
FREE* Tiny Phone

(guaranteed to fit in your dorm room – and your back pocket)

(phone model may vary)

+

- **FREE** Hands-free Kit
- **FREE** In-car Charger
- **FREE** Shipping and Handling

You choose the phone. You choose the plan.
whereverU puts you in control.
Wherever you are, you *can* stay in touch.

whereverU
please stay in touch.

Use our rate comparison wizard to choose the plan that's right for you

www.whereverU.com/eyn or call **1.800.300.7066**

mention bonus code: 15770

Plans available from:

NEXTEL

Step 1: Get two FREE* phones. One for you, one for Mom and Dad.

Step 2: Learn to use caller ID.

(phone model may vary)

VoiceStream FamilyTime™ Plan from whereverU

- **FREE*** Nationwide Long Distance.
- **FREE*** Nationwide Roaming.
- **UNLIMITED*** calls to any VoiceStream phone – anytime.

2 FREE* phones,
One bill they'll be happy to pay.

wherever you are, you *can* stay in touch.

Global Wireless by **T··Mobile··**

Authorized Dealer

usually includes free long-distance and roaming within a cluster of states, such as New England or the entire Northeast. Lastly, for those whose homes and schools are on opposite sides of the country, the nationwide plans let this all happen on a national scale.

What is local or regional will vary depending on which service provider and plan you're considering. For the best information, check out the websites of various service providers, where you will find highlighted maps displaying different coverage areas.

Do I Want Analog Or Digital?

Your location also impacts what type of service is better for you: analog or digital. All cell phone service used to be analog, so that means you can use it to make calls from pretty much anywhere. But digital service is quickly catching up, having grown out of a concentration in urban areas. Therefore, if you're going to be spending a lot of time in rural areas, an analog plan may be your best (or only) option. Otherwise, try a digital package, because:

- The sound quality of digital service is generally better.

- Digital uses less power than analog, so the phones and batteries are smaller and you get more talk time out of your battery life.

- Digital service offers a greater choice of phones and features

If you're going to school in an urban area but want the option of roaming into analog areas, try a digital plan with a dual-band phone. This will allow you to use analog networks if you stray outside your digital service area. Be careful—this can be expensive. (You'll learn more about selecting a phone later in this chapter.)

When And How Much Will I Use My Phone?

One very important thing to consider in selecting a service plan is when and how much you are going to be using your phone. Monthly plans are usually sold in blocks of minutes, from less than 30 to thousands per month. Unless you get an "anytime" plan that allows you to use your block of minutes whenever you want, your airtime will be broken up into "peak" and "off-peak" minutes. You will usually get fewer peak minutes, which are generally from 7 a.m. to 7 p.m. on weekdays (actual times vary depending on service providers), but many more of the "off-peak" minutes, also referred to as night and weekend minutes, for all other times of the day. The good news is that this is usually not a problem for college students, who as a group do most of their calling later in the evening or on weekends anyway!

Want to save some minutes?

Find out if you can check your voice mail by calling your cell number from a traditional phone (land line).

Be realistic about how you will use your phone. It is very expensive if you use more peak minutes than you have in your plan, so you may want to keep track of how many you've used during a month. You can do this by checking your account on your service provider's website or by tracking it directly on your phone (some carriers provide this service). On the other hand, you also don't want to want to sign up for a plan with more minutes than you'll actually use. You may want to experiment with a more conservative plan. If you find you need more minutes, your service provider will usually be happy to upgrade you. Just don't start too big, since they typically won't let you go down.

How Much Do I Want To Spend?

So now you know what you want, but how much can you afford? Certainly you can control your spending with a prepaid plan, but on a monthly plan you need to be a little more careful. Each month, you will pay:

Monthly fee: When shopping for monthly plans you will get a good idea for how much you will spend by looking at the monthly fee for the plan. Just make sure you know what this includes since, as you will see, other charges can add up quickly!

Added features: It is important to know what your monthly fee includes and how that compares to the features you want. Depending on your plan, certain services may or may not be included in the monthly fee, such as: voice mail, call-waiting, call forwarding, voice-activated dialing, text messaging, and wireless Web. If you're interested in any extra services, find out how much more they will cost you. Some new services that providers are trying to encourage may come free with your plan for a certain period of time. If so, make sure you know when you will be expected to pick up the tab. You may get free Web access for six months, but then the charge could go up to something as high as an additional $10 per month.

In addition to what you will pay each month, you could also be subject to the following one-time charges:

Activation fee: When you sign up for new service, there is an activation fee. Sometimes as part of a promotion, this fee will be waived. If not, expect to pay about $25.

Cancellation fee: When you sign up for a plan, make sure you can make the commitment. As mentioned earlier, most monthly plans will require a one- or two-year service contract. Once you sign, you will be expected to remain with your service provider, paying your monthly bill, for that amount of time. If you change your mind, you will be required to pay a hefty cancellation fee, often hundreds of dollars!

Phones

There are so many different makes and models of cell phones on the market that it's impossible to keep track of them all. It's also safe to say that about two weeks after you get your phone (absolutely the best phone in the world, you think), there will be a newer, nicer, smaller, and more powerful one out there. When shopping for a phone, you need to think about:

How much you can pay: There's a lot of variation in how much you could pay for a cell phone depending on how new and small you want it to be and how many features you want it to have. At the low end, you can often get a cell phone for free as part of a promotion when signing up for a new service plan. Usually these free phones are slightly older models that they're looking to clear from the shelves, and you'll need to submit rebates to get your money back. On the high end, you can spend hundreds of dollars on the perfect phone/PDA combo. When deciding what to pay, think about what is important to you and before you spend a lot of money, remember that cell phones can be easily lost or broken and that if you ever decide to change your service provider you will probably need to buy a new one.

Which service provider you selected: Many phones only work on one company's plans, largely because each service provider uses slightly different technologies. So before you get your heart set on a specific phone, make sure it is compatible with the plan and provider you chose. Although some phones can be transferred between companies, most cannot.

If you have analog or digital service: You will need to buy a phone that works with the type of technology your service uses, analog or digital. If you sign up for analog service, you should think about buying a phone that that is dual-band since it will work on your analog service and it will be able to work on a digital network, too, in case your service provider upgrades while you're on your plan. If you're on digital service you can buy either a digital phone or one that is dual-band. While digital-only will suffice, having a dual-band phone will provide you with the option of roaming onto a analog network if you're ever traveling out of your service area and need to use your phone.

Size: Do you want a teeny-tiny phone to fit in your purse or pants pocket? Or does size not really matter? A small phone may be light and portable, but it might have short battery life, miniscule buttons, and a small screen to go with it. Consider the

PHONE HOME

I got my first cell phone when I was a senior at MIT. My dorm didn't offer long-distance service, so I'd been making all my calls using a calling card my parents gave me when I left for school. The card was associated with my parents' long-distance plan, and until one month when we got a bill for $100, none of us realized that the rates we were paying were outrageous! I'm sure not all cards are so bad, but after our $100 bill we figured out that we'd been paying nearly $1 a minute for long distance! Shocked, I began looking into alternatives.

What I found was that some cell phone plans offered "free" long distance. It didn't matter where in the country I was calling, or from where I was calling. I would just pay a flat monthly rate for a preset number of minutes, and long-distance was included. This was perfect for calling my parents from school and also for times when I was traveling out of town, like during spring break.

There were also other advantages to having a cell phone. I felt better walking home late at night knowing I had my phone in case of emergency. Also, since I took my phone everywhere, I no longer worried about missing important calls if I was out of my room. And I started screening calls so I wouldn't get caught up in unimportant conversations when I had tons of work to do.

In addition to all the reasons I loved my cell phone, I know my parents appreciated it, too. As an architecture major it was common for me to stay in the studio until 4 a.m., but with my cell phone, my parents could get hold of me no matter where I was (and vice versa) at a decent hour. This also helped them break their habit of calling my room early on Saturday mornings. Thinking about all the sleep I lost and the conveniences my cell phone provides, makes me wish I had gotten one much sooner.

— Jennifer M., Massachusetts Institute of Technology

trade-offs between the size of the phone, its features and how easy it is for you to use—and lose.

Battery life: A phone won't do you much good if its battery is always dead. Look for a phone with a battery life that fits your schedule. The longer the battery life, the longer you can go without recharging.

If you're interested in text messaging, you should know that currently, in order to send someone a text message on their phone, they must use the same service provider as you do for them to receive it. If you use Sprint and your pal uses Cingular, no dice!

Features: Make sure that your phone is capable of performing any features you ordered as a part of your plan. For instance, if you register for a plan that lets you send your sweetie text messages while you're in class, you'd better buy a phone that's capable of delivering on that promise. Other features to keep in mind include ring type (you'll want a vibrating option for when you have your phone on during lecture) and Web-readiness. If you get Web access on your plan you'll want a phone that is capable of connecting, with big buttons and a large display that allow you to make the most of this feature.

Getting Started

So you've done your research and you know you want a cell phone. At this point, generally, the procedure is to buy a cell phone and a service plan at the same time. There are many ways to do this:

Direct from the service provider: If you're pretty sure which carrier you want to use, one way to sign up for service and get your phone is to go straight to the source: one of the websites or retail stores that belong to the various service providers. If you go into one of the stores, you can have all your questions answered by someone knowledgeable about the company's plans, and you can play with the phones you are considering. Or, if you don't live near one of the stores, service providers also

offer a lot of information on their websites. Then, you can conveniently buy your phone and set up your new service either in person at the store or online over the Internet.

Third-party stores: If you're still trying to decide between service providers, it might be good for you to go somewhere that you can learn more about the various providers and compare them. One way to do this is to go to one of the many electronics, office superstores, and cell-phone shops or kiosks that are authorized dealers of multiple phones and plans. Here, the advantage is that you can talk to a salesperson about your various options (not just one like in the store of a service provider) and kick the tires on prospective phones.

Third-party online retailers: Similar to the third-party stores, but online, these websites are also authorized dealers for the main cell phone companies. If you don't want to go into a store and talk to someone, often these websites offer you a visual table or grid for easy comparison between plans and phones from different companies. If you're comfortable shopping online, this can be a convenient way to set up your new service.

E-MAIL & INSTANT MESSAGING

Over the past few years, e-mail has become an indispensable part of life, especially for college students. E-mail is often the most convenient way to communicate with friends, family, potential employers, professors, college administrators, and just about everyone else. Some students now even receive their college acceptance letters via e-mail!

Instant messaging (IM) has grown too; IMs are constantly popping up on computer screens at campuses across the nation. Many students find that IM can't be beat for spur-of-the-moment plans or spontaneous conversations.

College E-Mail Account

Your college will give you an address that resembles student@yourschool.edu probably sometime before you move to campus, either upon acceptance or over the summer. Whenever your school gives this to you, start using it. Share your new address with friends and family as soon as you have it to let them know how to get in touch with you once you move.

Even if you have another e-mail address, like an AOL, Yahoo!, or Hotmail account, your college address should become your primary account once you receive it. At school, this account will be like your virtual identity and a crucial lifeline to the rest of the college community, delivering important news about classes, school policies, recruiting, and social events. You may even use it to log on to different services around campus, from public computers to college housing applications. Furthermore, it's a great way to identify yourself as a student when signing up for services and receiving student discounts online.

Most colleges will not let you choose your own user name, although a few will. Sometimes, it's actually more convenient for students to be assigned e-mail addresses. When everyone's e-mail follows the same exact format, such as firstname_lastname@yourschool.edu, you don't have to guess at addresses. However, if you go to a school that allows you to pick your username, choose wisely. Your friends might think mac_daddy@yourschool.edu is funny, but job recruiters probably won't.

When using your college e-mail account, keep in mind:

Even though you're on e-mail 24 hours a day, your professors may not be: For any professor-types who seem less than technologically adventurous, you may want to follow up your e-mail messages to them with phone calls or office visits.

Don't abuse your e-mail account: Most schools have strict policies regarding spam, harassment, and commercial use.

Don't open any attachments sent to you unless you know what it is and who sent it: School mail systems may take precautions to eliminate the risk that you will receive a virus through your e-mail, but it's better to be safe than sorry!

Don't play games with e-mail: You might think it's funny when someone uses your roommate's computer to send out an embarrassing e-mail from his account, but you won't be laughing if it happens to you...

Home E-Mail Account

In addition to your college account, if you already have an e-mail address you've been using at home you will likely want to keep it. This way, you won't miss any e-mails that would be sent there, like those from old friends to whom you forgot to give your new address, or e-mail newsletters you may have requested.

Keeping your home account may also give you a way to access your college e-mail when you are off the college network. If your college e-mail is not Web-based, meaning that you cannot check it from anywhere that you have Internet access, find out if you can forward your college e-mail to your home account.

That way you won't miss any important e-mails when you are off campus, like when you are home for Thanksgiving or winter break.

Connecting To Your E-Mail Account

Virtually all colleges provide their students with free campus Internet access to check e-mail and go online. If you live in a dorm and have your own computer, you'll probably even have high-speed Internet access through the college network. In addition, most schools have public computers set up around campus for students to use.

If you live off campus, your college may offer a way to dial into its network using a modem. Otherwise, you'll need to set up your own Internet access. Traditional dial-up service is still usually the cheapest way to connect. For a faster connection, consider broadband services such as cable or DSL.

Once you have a connection to the Internet, how you receive your e-mail may depend on whether or not your college uses a Web-based system. If they do, checking your e-mail will be as easy as going to the Web address (URL) for your school's mail system and logging in to your account.

Alternatively, if your school does not have a Web-based way to access your mail, you should receive information from your school about configuring your e-mail software to send and receive messages using your college account. For additional information on e-mail software, please refer to Chapter 2.

Instant Messaging

Many college students use IM services like AOL IM, Yahoo! Messenger, MSN Messenger, and ICQ to carry on conversations with friends: chatting, making plans for dinner, or exchanging study tips.

PACKING CHECKLIST

❏ = Essential   ❍ = Optional

Bedding

❏ Pillow and pillowcases
❏ Sheets and blankets (extra-long if needed)
❏ Comforter, quilt, or bed-spread
❍ Mattress pad
❍ Egg crate, body pillow, or feather bed
❍ Sleeping bag

Furniture & Decorations

❍ Chair: inflatable, folding or bean bag
❍ Couch or futon
❍ Packing trunk (makeshift coffee table)
❍ Full-length mirror
❍ Plastic storage bins
❍ Crates
❍ Bulletin board
❍ White board, pen, and eraser
❍ String of holiday lights
❍ Doorbell
❍ Plant
❍ Baskets (for holding stuff)
❍ Rug and doormat
❍ Wall tapestry
❏ Trash can and bags
❍ Posters and poster tape
❍ Other creative wall deco-rations

Appliances & Electronics

❏ Mini-refrigerator
❏ Extension cords
❏ Alarm clock
❏ Portable phone
❍ Answering machine
❍ TV and VCR or DVD
❍ VHS tapes or DVDs
❏ Lamps: floor, desk and bedside
❍ Stereo
❍ Headphones
❍ CD collection
❍ Portable music player
❍ Cell phone
❍ Fan
❍ Hotpot, microwave, and toaster (if allowed)
❍ Videogame console
❍ Small vacuum cleaner

Computing

❏ Computer
❍ Printer
❍ Printer cable
❍ Replacement ink cartridges
❍ Printer paper
❍ Blank disks or CDs
❏ Surge protector
❏ Computer manuals and

installation disks
- ○ Mouse and mouse pad
- ○ Phone cord for modem
- ○ Personal Digital Assistant
- ○ Digital camera
- ○ Speakers

Other Essentials

- ❏ Laundry hamper
- ❏ Clothes hangers
- ○ Shoe rack
- ❏ Detergent, fabric softener, and stain stick
- ○ Fabric deodorizer
- ○ Drying rack
- ○ Iron
- ❏ Quarters
- ❏ Bathroom caddy
- ○ Hairdryer
- ❏ Towels and washcloths
- ❏ Mini first-aid kit (bandages, antibiotic cream, pain reliever, upset stomach medicine, thermometer, and decongestants)
- ❏ Prescription medication
- ❏ Eyeglasses or contacts
- ❏ Contact lens solution
- ❏ Shampoo and conditioner
- ❏ Soap or body wash
- ❏ Toothpaste and brush
- ❏ Dental floss
- ○ Vitamins
- ○ Cosmetics
- ❏ Deodorant
- ○ Skin cream
- ❏ Razors
- ○ Shaving cream
- ○ Acne cream

- ○ Lip balm
- ○ Mouthwash
- ❏ Nail clippers
- ❏ Brush or comb
- ○ Q-tips and cotton balls
- ○ Sunscreen
- ○ Hair accessories
- ○ Feminine hygiene products
- ❏ Tissues
- ○ Earplugs
- ❏ Ziploc bags

Books & Supplies

- ❏ Backpack or school bag
- ○ Calendar
- ○ Day planner
- ○ Desk organizer
- ❏ Address book
- ○ Stamps
- ○ Stationery or notecards
- ○ Envelopes
- ❏ Calculator
- ❏ Batteries
- ○ Camera and film
- ❏ 3-ring binders
- ❏ Folders
- ❏ Notebooks
- ❏ Index cards
- ○ Paper clips
- ○ Rubber bands
- ❏ Pencils, pens, and highlighters
- ○ Pencil sharpener
- ○ Ruler
- ○ Thumbtacks
- ○ Post-It notes
- ○ Scissors
- ○ Tape
- ○ Stapler and staples

- ○ Wite-Out
- ○ Photo album (one full and one empty)
- ○ High school yearbook
- ○ Reference texts: dictionary, thesaurus, grammar and style guide, quotation book, and foreign language dictionary
- ❏ *Everything You Need For College* (This book!)

Clothing

- ❏ Underwear
- ❏ Undershirts
- ❏ Socks: dress, athletic, and casual
- ❏ Jeans
- ❏ Khakis
- ❏ Shorts
- ❏ Skirts
- ❏ Shirts
- ❏ Sweaters
- ❏ Dresses
- ❏ T-shirts
- ❏ Sweats and sweatshirts
- ❏ Workout clothes
- ❏ Pajamas
- ○ Robe
- ○ Slippers
- ❏ Shower flip-flops
- ❏ Shoes: dress, athletic, and casual
- ❏ Belts
- ❏ Pantyhose and tights
- ❏ Hats
- ❏ Purses
- ○ Jewelry
- ❏ Light or rain jacket
- ❏ Winter jacket

- ❏ Boots
- ○ Gloves or mittens
- ❏ Umbrella
- ❏ Bathing suit
- ❏ Dress pants
- ❏ Sports jacket
- ❏ Ties
- ❏ Evening bag
- ❏ Evening dress
- ❏ Suit

Miscellaneous

- ○ Sporting equipment (frisbee, softball glove, balls, skis, racquets, etc.)
- ○ Travel sewing kit
- ○ Mini toolkit (hammer, nails, screwdrivers, and tape measure)
- ❏ Flashlight
- ○ Dishes, cups, and utensils
- ○ Bottle and can openers
- ○ Cleaning supplies (glass cleaner, dish soap, and air freshener)
- ○ Favorite snack food, soda, candy, and gum
- ○ Water filter and pitcher
- ○ Light bulbs
- ○ Batteries

MOVING
& TRAVEL

MOVING

C hances are you're going to want to bring a lot of
stuff with you to school, but you should try to live
without all 40 pairs of shoes, 20 stuffed animals,
and 200 CDs. As if deciding which ones to bring
won't be a tough enough issue, you're also going to have to
figure out how to move everything without breaking it. This
chapter spells out how to best pack, ship, move, and store
your most valuable possessions.

PACKING

The first step in packing is choosing containers. There are
a lot of options—trunks, suitcases, boxes, trash bags, and
crates will litter the halls of every dormitory on move-in

day. While crates and trash bags are good for switching rooms during the semester, there are better options for your initial move to campus.

Boxes: These are probably the best packing containers because they're cheap, collapsible, and reusable. First, check your attic and basement for old boxes. After that, good bets for finding free boxes outside the house include the supermarket, home superstores, and liquor stores. If you're not up to the challenge of scavenging around town to save a few bucks, you can always buy. New boxes are clean, sturdy, and you don't have to pull them out of a dumpster. Buy new boxes at any box store, moving truck rental company, or office supply store. They're usually sold alone or in various-sized packs. If you need anything larger than the smallest pack, you're probably bringing too much with you to school; the average dorm room is only 100 to 200 square feet, so you can't pack too much in there. Don't forget to pick up some bubble wrap, foam peanuts, packing tape, and a marker, too.

Trunks: Want to look glamorous arriving at school with a caravan of trunks following you? Better think again. Traveling like royalty might seem like fun at first, but who do you think is going to be lugging all those trunks up four flights of stairs? (You, of course.) And besides, any sophomore can tell you that you won't have anywhere to keep the trunks after you unpack. One trunk is fine, since it can do double-duty as a coffee table, but everything else you pack in should be collapsible.

Luggage: If you are considering buying new luggage for your move, invest in a large suitcase with wheels, a carry-on with wheels, a large duffel bag, and a backpack. If you choose carefully, you'll be able to put the duffel bag inside the carry-on rolling bag, and the carry-on rolling bag inside the large rolling bag, so when you arrive at school your luggage won't take up much room. If you're lucky, it will fit right under your bed. Even if you're not flying to college, it's a good idea to buy luggage that will comply with airline policies so you can use it later. To learn more about airline-friendly luggage and flying for your move to campus, take a trip to Chapter 6, Travel.

Protecting What You Pack

Once you decide what you're using to pack, make sure it's protected. This means protecting it from loss, would-be thieves, and accidental breakage. Having your stereo stolen en route to campus will start your college experience off on the wrong foot. And the only thing worse than having it stolen is finding it in a million itty-bitty pieces when it gets there. To avoid this and equally horrifying tragedies, follow these packing tips:

Be original: Many times when you're traveling with luggage and a bag is "stolen," someone else has just accidentally mistaken it for their own. To avoid confusion, place a unique, bright marking on your luggage (try knotting a colorful bandanna to the handle) to help it stand out in a crowd.

Add a lock: To prevent those people who aren't mistaking your bags for theirs and are taking them anyway, get locks for your luggage. Although locks may draw attention to your baggage (Look! I'm protecting something valuable!) they make getting into your suitcase that much more difficult, discouraging would-be thieves from messing with your stuff.

Label everything: Clearly writing your name, address, and telephone number can get a missing item returned to you quickly; adding a description of contents to that label can mean it never gets returned. Don't publicize that a certain box is carrying your CD collection or your new DVD player.

Choose the right box: When you're packing a heavy and fragile item like your stereo or computer monitor, use its original box, which is the perfect size and durability, if possible. If you've thrown away the original box, use a double-walled box. You can make one by packing the item into a box, then packing that box into another box with a layer of foam peanuts in between.

Be a lightweight: Don't just toss everything you own into one huge box—you'll never be able to lift it, or the bottom will come crashing out! Keep the weight of each box under 50 pounds, even less if you are unable to lift that amount easily or need to make repeated trips up stairs. The heavier the items you're packing, the smaller the box you should use. And by all means, whatever the weight of the box, seal it with strong tape. This means duct tape or plastic moving tape that's at least 2 to 3 inches wide to properly seal the flaps—not masking or Scotch. And remember, lift with your knees, not your back!

Add padding: When selecting boxes for breakable items, make sure they are large enough to put adequate padding around their contents, and durable enough to ensure that they won't collapse. Wrap fragile items separately with old newspaper, bubble wrap, sheets, blankets, T-shirts, pillows, or towels. If you're shipping several items in one box, after wrapping them separately, fill in the spaces between them with at least two to three inches of packing material. This will minimize movement inside the box during transit, so your items have a better chance of arriving intact.

Get help: If you don't think you can pack your boxes properly, you should use a packing professional. You may pay a little more for their services than if you packed yourself, but you will save time and won't have to worry about your items arriving undamaged. To find the nearest shipping outlet, check out the local mall, or let your fingers do the walking by checking the Yellow Pages or online.

SHIPPING

If you won't be able to bring all of your belongings with you on your trip, shipping a portion of them is a relatively hassle-free option. A variety of companies can ship your belongings, the three largest being the U. S. Postal Service, Federal Express, and United Parcel Service.

Ultimately, how you decide to ship your belongings will depend on how far you're shipping them, how much you have, how heavy the boxes are, how soon you need them, and how much you can spend. Here are some tips for a good shipping experience:

Call ahead: Although you may already know your dorm room address, your college may have a different address for shipping belongings prior to arrival. Check with your school and ask whether they will hold boxes for you before you arrive. While some campuses will hold your belongings for a few days, others will not. If they will hold boxes, time them to arrive one to two days before you arrive. If they won't, time them to arrive one to two days later, and you can pick them up at the local post office.

Consider the ground option: It will take about 5 to 7 days for your packages to reach their destination, but it's generally the least expensive method.

Label with care: To give your box a better chance of arriving as scheduled, position the address label squarely on the largest surface. Avoid wrinkles, rips, stains, or stray marks on labels, and don't draw a pretty border or anything else around it. If possible, include a phone number where you can be reached on campus in case something happens.

Be insured: Insurance is an additional cost, but it's well worth it if your packages get lost or damaged. Insurance costs about $2 for up to $100 in valuables, and an extra $1 for each additional $100 of value. The maximum coverage per box is usually $5,000 (and you shouldn't be bringing anything worth $5,000 to campus). You won't get extra money for sentimental losses, so if you can't imagine living without something forever, live without it for a year and leave it at home.

SHIP IT!

During my first two years of college I took pride in the fact that I always managed to fit everything I needed into my car. However, during my junior year I accumulated a lot of stuff and when packing up after finals, I soon realized that despite successfully unloading luxury items like halogen lamps and old dirty fans on the other residents in my dorm, I was still not able to fit everything into my little two-door car.

Although driving five hours with a mini-fridge on my lap was not the best idea, I thought about it! I had no choice but to enlist some friends to help me. We spent quite awhile rearranging and strategically placing items, but there just wasn't enough space. With nothing else to do, I tossed my remaining possessions into a big box and borrowed a friend's car to drive to a shipping outlet in town.

Once at the store, I placed my heavy box on the counter. When the clerk finished laughing at me, he suggested we repack the box so that nothing would break or be damaged. He went to work utilizing those crazy foam peanuts and several sheets of bubble wrap. In no time he had the whole thing packed, sealed, and ready for shipment! I was impressed, to say the least! At the last minute, I even opted for the extra insurance—it only cost a few bucks but more than covered the contents.

Later that evening I arrived home in one piece. I wish I could say the same for the box. When it arrived a few days later, it had suffered some acute trauma en route. I quickly opened it to see if my stereo equipment was broken. To my surprise, there was no damage to the contents, thanks to the superb packaging job done by the clerk. If he hadn't taken the time to pack it properly and remind me about the extra insurance, I would have certainly lost more than $350. Using a shipping outlet is definitely a good idea when you have to send something!

— Scott N., Lafayette College

MOVERS

Not feeling up to the challenge of moving? You can always get someone else to do it for you. No, you don't have to make your dad or big brother carry your stuff. (Although that could be a good idea.) Instead, figure out if hiring a moving company is a good idea. When investigating this option, beware that it's usually significantly more expensive than doing it yourself (or making your dad do it), and that you'll need to do your homework. Ask friends and family for recommendations, check the phone directory, and look at online moving resources for more information. Then, when making your decision, follow these five tips:

Get estimates: Approach several moving companies for an estimate of how much your move will cost. Local moves are generally billed at an hourly rate, ranging anywhere from $80 to $200 per hour. This generally includes a truck and the labor of two or three men for at least three hours. If your move is going to be long-distance, the charges will probably be based on the weight of the goods you are moving and the distance they're going. Try to avoid any mover with a weight minimum;

Many companies will require you to pay for moving at least 1,000 pounds of stuff, much more than you'll have. Then, look at how much they're charging you per mile.

Try a college specialist: Some companies specialize in college moving. You'll have to pack and load your belongings yourself, but you'll only pay for the actual space you use in the truck. The rest of it will be shared with other students. A professional driver will deliver your belongings to campus for you, but you'll be responsible for unloading them yourself. So, you do the bulk of the work, but you don't have to worry about transporting everything, and the cost is usually only marginally more expensive than a truck rental.

Pack yourself: Even if your mover offers to pack all of your belongings, it's often very expensive. However, since movers aren't responsible for anything that breaks in a box they didn't pack, use some of the money you save to buy supplemental insurance that covers the boxes you packed.

Ask about insurance: Basic insurance included with your move usually only provides 30 to 60 cents of coverage for each pound transported, so if your $300, 10-pound television is dropped during the move, you're only going to get $3 to $6 for it from the moving company. Since $3 doesn't come close to getting you a new TV, consider purchasing supplemental insurance. More commonly known as renter's insurance, it will not only cover your move, it will also cover your belongings while you're at school. For more information on buying insurance, be sure to read Chapter 9.

Get it in writing: Ask your moving company for a written contract prior to moving day, and be sure you understand it before signing. If it doesn't specify every little detail (such as mileage, packing, standard charges, additional costs, and insurance), insist on adding these items to the contract.

STORAGE

You might wonder why you need to know about storage before you even get to campus, but you do. First of all, you might want to know what your options are in case you overpack and everything doesn't fit in your room. (Who knew four boxes of sweaters would be too many?) Secondly, you'll want to think ahead to what happens over summer break—storage space often disappears quickly. You don't want to be thrown out of your dorm room on the last day of finals with nowhere to stick your stuff for the summer and no money to ship it home.

On Campus

Your options for storage vary depending on where you go to school, but many colleges will provide space during the term or when you're off campus, either over summer break or doing a semester abroad.

During the school year you probably won't need much storage space, but if your room is really cramped, you may be able to keep a box or two in the basement of your building. During winter break, almost all colleges will allow you to leave your items in your room, so you won't need to worry about anything then.

Over the summer or during a semester away, most colleges will not allow you to keep anything in your room because they will be renting it out to another boarder. However, in some cases, they will provide an area in a dorm basement or another on-campus facility where you can keep your books, bedding, winter clothes, and other non-valuable items. If you're lucky, they will also provide a high-security area where you can keep your bike, stereo, computer, and other valuables.

Off Campus

Storage space is a luxury that not all colleges provide. Even if they do, they're not responsible for anything lost or damaged. Because of this, you may find yourself deciding between storage or shipping your stuff home each summer. Depending on how far away you live and what kind of transportation you have, this could be a big inconvenience and an even bigger expense. If this is the case, look into renting an off-campus space to stash your stuff.

When looking for storage:

Visit first: Before deciding on a place to store your belongings, it's good to take a trip there to check it out. Shoot for a decent neighborhood and make sure access to the facility is controlled (there is a locked gate or security codes are required).

Ask about the weather: If you're going to be storing electronic equipment, make sure the space is climate-controlled (heated in the winter and air-conditioned in the summer).

Call your insurance: Check whether your existing insurance policy will cover your items in storage. If not, be sure you purchase additional insurance from the storage location itself.

Reserve early: Chances are that a 5'x5' storage space will fit all your clothes, as well as your computer, bike, books, and anything else you might want to leave at school. You would only need more space to store large items like furniture. The catch is that since this size space fits all your stuff, chances are it will fit most other students' stuff just fine too, which means these rooms will go first. Secure your space early, so you don't end up having to pay for a bigger room than you need.

Plan your route: Figure out how you'll get your stuff into storage ahead of time. Consider how far the facility is from campus. If you have a car or can borrow one for a few hours, this may not a problem. Otherwise, decide if a taxi is a viable idea.

CHAPTER SIX

TRAVEL

There's no doubt about it: If you go to school away from home, you're going to be doing a lot of traveling during your college career. First, there's the trip to school. Then, there are trips home at Thanksgiving, winter recess, and probably during the summer, too. And let's not forget spring break, which is likely to be your favorite college travel experience.

So if you're not already a seasoned traveler, you will be by the time you get your diploma. This chapter will teach you the finer points of travel, including how to get the best deals on airline tickets, tips for driving to campus, and how to save on a hotel room even when you don't have a reservation.

TRAVEL AGENTS

Unlike most travelers, you won't need an agent's advice on where to go—that was your high school guidance counselor's job. But whether you've decided to go to school just across the state line or all the way across the country, using an agent to book your trip can save you time and money. A good agent can offer many helpful services (provided for free or for a small charge, so ask!), including:

Being an expert: Travel agents plan trips for a living, so they know more about it than you do. Agents receive faxes, e-mails, and phone calls every day that allow them to stay on top of current promotions. Work with them and you'll be in the know, too.

Why is it so important to get a good deal?

According to the folks at collegeboard.com, travel accounts for about 25% of an average student's discretionary spending! That's a lot of dough!

Working for you: Travel agents provide you with suggestions that are in your best interest because you're the boss. And since they know that the cheapest is not always the best, they'll be able to tell you if a too-good-to-be-true deal really is too good to be true.

Increasing the size of the fine print: A good agent will make you aware of any cancellation penalties or restrictions imposed on your trip. Understanding the fine print can save you money and a headache should you need to change your itinerary.

Resolving problems: Your travel agent is also your personal bodyguard. In the event that something goes wrong, they might not help you bust a kneecap, but they will do everything in their power to fix the problem. And because agents refer a lot of businesses to the airlines, their complaints will carry more weight than yours would.

Finding An Agent

Now that you know how valuable a travel agent can be, it's time to locate one. If your family already has one it likes, call that agent to plan your trip. If not, you should ask someone you trust to refer you to a reliable agent, or find one yourself in the phone directory, online, or in this book. In your search, you may want to consider looking for an agency that specializes in student travel.

Instead of (or in addition to) finding a conventional travel agent, investigate using an online travel website. These have proved reliable and relatively easy to use to research travel, compare prices, and make reservations, so it's no surprise that they're gaining in popularity.

Rest assured that buying a ticket online is pretty much the same thing as buying one through a travel agency, except you probably won't have someone to call for help should problems arise. Don't be afraid to buy a ticket online, just know what you're getting into and be aware of any restrictions.

FLYING

"Hello, this is Captain Johnson speaking. On behalf of my crew, I'd like to welcome you aboard West-East Airways Flight 302 from Los Angeles to Boston. We are currently leveling off at an altitude of 35,000 feet. If you look out the windows on the starboard side of the aircraft, you will see your parents waving goodbye in the distance.

A FLIGHT TO FORGET

I chose to go to school far from home, and during my freshman year I got very homesick. This was especially true around the holidays, so I was psyched when I was able to convince my mom to fly me home for Thanksgiving.

In her infinite wisdom, my mother used a travel agent to book my flight. The agent sent my tickets and itinerary directly to my dorm address, making it all very convenient. All I had to do was pack and make it to the airport on time. That should've been easy enough.

My flight was booked for 7 a.m. the Wednesday before Thanksgiving. Although I was looking forward to going home, I hated leaving my boyfriend and roommate, so I stayed up talking to them nearly the entire night before my flight. Eventually, with my bag already packed and ready for a quick getaway the next morning, I decided to get some sleep to avoid complete exhaustion.

The next thing I remember was waking up at 10 a.m. and feeling confused. I couldn't figure out what was going on because it was sunny outside, but I was supposed to leave in the dark, early hours of the morning. Suddenly I jumped to my feet. I had slept though my alarm and missed my flight!

I panicked. My first reaction was to contact my mom, but a call home confirmed that she had already left for the day. Then, holding my itinerary in my hand, I noticed that the phone number of the travel agent was in bold at the top of the page. I decided to call and to my surprise, someone actually answered the phone on the busiest travel day of the year!

The agent, Becky, calmed me down and said she would contact the airline and attempt to put me on the next available flight. She came through with a similar flight the following day, and most importantly, I didn't have to pay for a new ticket. That Thanksgiving I was thankful to have a travel agent as resourceful and experienced as Becky on my side!

— Ann B., Syracuse University

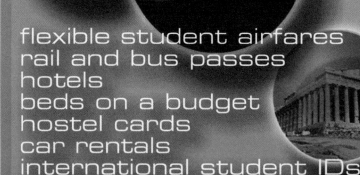

Congratulations, you're now officially a college student. We should be arriving at your new home in approximately five and a half hours."

There are countless ways to get from point A to point B, and your decision to take a plane, bus, train, or automobile will definitely give your trip to school a different flavor. Of all the modes of transportation available, flying is usually the quickest, so if you're in a hurry to leave high school behind and become the BMOC (that's Big Man On Campus, for those of you who aren't yet used to college lingo), it might be the best option for you. However, no matter how much of a hurry you're in, you should consider the different costs and luggage restrictions before deciding on the best way to make your first trip to school, especially if you're not traveling far.

Should you decide that air travel is the best option for you, follow these pointers to get the best rate possible on your flight to school:

Reserve early: Make your reservation as soon as you know what day you want to arrive. Airlines give discounts for bookings made at least 21 days in advance.

Shop around: Shopping online can be the quickest way to compare rates from many different airlines and find the best deal. Then, check your findings with a travel agent you trust. If they find a better bargain than you did, you'll be reassured that you're receiving the best deal out there. If they don't, you can just book the deal you found online originally.

Be flexible: Do you absolutely *have* to be at school on the 20th instead of the 19th? For big savings, be flexible about the day and time you travel. Flights in the middle of the week, either early in the morning or late at night, are usually the least expensive.

Take an indirect route: Having a stopover (or two or three) can save you money over flying direct. Just make sure that the extra savings are worth the extra hassle.

Buy the whole package: Check into booking the flight as a package deal if your parents are traveling with you. If you purchase their hotel room and rental car at the same time as your airfare, you'll probably get a discount.

Ask for a student discount: Many airlines don't publicize their student rates, so when you're making your reservation be sure to ask if there are any. Many airlines will give you a significant discount just for showing your student ID, and others allow you to fly stand-by for an even lower rate. If you don't have your student ID in time for your first trip to school, but still want the student discount, airlines will also accept an International Student Identification Card (ISIC) that you can get for about $20 from a travel agent. Or, some airlines will give you the discount simply for being college-aged (under 23).

Traveling to NY? You might want to bring a book...

The Federal Aviation Administration reports that the following airports have the worst delays: LaGuardia, Newark, O'Hare, San Francisco, Boston, Philadelphia, JFK, Atlanta, Houston and Dallas.

Fly somewhere else: You may be able to fly into an airport at a city neighboring your school for a much lower rate, so check out flights to alternate destinations. Just remember to allow for other costs when you consider this option. If you pay $275 for a flight to Providence instead of $300 for a flight to Boston, you still might have to take a $30 bus ride to your final destination. Make sure you're not down five bucks and an hour-long bus ride if you decide to fly to an alternate airport.

Fly frequently: Frequent Flyer programs are a good way to get a free ticket, a better seat, or even a class upgrade. Join a frequent flyer program (or two or three or six) before you leave, so you can start collecting points on your first trip to school.

Charge it: Keep an eye out for credit card companies that offer travel discounts to students. Some offer free tickets when you apply, exclusive rates when you use your card on a particular airline, or frequent flyer points when you make purchases—even if they're not travel-related.

Get bumped: If there are less than eight seats left when you make a reservation, someone will probably get bumped from the flight. Getting bumped would be a disaster for business travelers, but for a carefree college student like you, getting bumped (and compensated) on purpose is one of the best ways to save on airfare. If you are bumped, there's a good chance you'll get a free ticket anywhere the airline flies, in addition to getting your original ticket for free. At the very least, you'll get a $50 voucher for traveling a couple of hours later. So book a ticket on a flight that's nearly full and you might get a free trip to Daytona Beach for spring break.

Luggage

You've probably flown before, but never with so many of your belongings! If you're flying to campus, it's important that you understand luggage restrictions so that you know what to bring along for the trip and what's better to ship.

The carry-on: The Federal Aviation Administration (FAA) limits passengers on U.S. flights to one carry-on bag and one personal article such as a purse or backpack. The size of your personal article can range from 14" to 16" high, 21" to 24" wide, and 8" to 9" deep, with the lower limits being for underseat storage, and the upper limits for the overhead compartment. Use this space wisely. If your checked baggage gets lost, you'll want to make sure you've packed these essentials in your carry-on:

- Your airline ticket and itinerary with confirmation numbers.

- Your passport, driver's license, or other valid photo ID.

- A wallet with a credit card, medical insurance card, and cash. (If you are bringing a lot of money with you, put some of it in traveler's checks.)

- A change of clothes, including extra underwear.

- Basic toiletries (toothbrush, toothpaste, deodorant, etc.) and any prescription medications.

- A portable music player, book, or other source of entertainment, plus your student orientation guide.

- Some snack food.

- Address, phone number, and directions to school.

What to check: Most airlines allow you to check two bags in addition to your carry-on items, but since luggage restrictions vary, you should ask your carrier for specifics.

As a rule of thumb, you're allowed two bags that weigh less than 70 pounds each. The weight of each bag matters. You can bring two 70-pound bags, but you cannot bring an 80-pound bag and a 20-pound bag. Since 70 pounds is pretty darn heavy, make sure these bags have wheels. Better to drag than carry. Furthermore, there are often restrictions on oversized or irregularly shaped items, so it might be easier to ship a bicycle than it would be to check it on the airplane.

All limits are now strictly enforced. Bags are weighed at check-in, security, and sometimes even the gate. So even if you've sneaked a bag on once, you won't necessarily get away with it this time. If your carry-on bag is too big, chances are you'll have to check it. If you've already checked the maximum number of bags, you'll be fined for bringing an extra bag.

If you plan to bring extra luggage, check with the airline first to see if they'll allow it on the plane. Even if you're willing to pay a fee (usually $75 to $100), they can still refuse your extra luggage if the plane is already full. If you receive permission ahead of time to bring your extra luggage, have the person granting you permission note it on your reservation, and be sure to get his or her name.

Baggage Claim

Examine your luggage carefully as soon as it comes off the carousel. If anything appears damaged or missing, report it to the airline before you leave the airport. The airline will trace missing baggage to let you know if it's just delayed, misrouted, or if it's really lost. You may not know the whereabouts of your luggage for several days, so be sure you have all the necessities in your carry-on bag. The airline will usually deliver luggage to you if it's found.

If your lost luggage is not found, you need to file a claim. Depending on the airline, you'll have three to five weeks to file, but the process isn't easy. You'll need to provide a list of all of the items in your bags, their cost, and when and where they were purchased. After the paperwork has been completed, it can take months to actually receive a check. To top it all off, in the U.S., the maximum airline reimbursement is only $1,250 per person, no matter how many bags were lost, and electronics, cameras, laptops, jewelry, and money are sometimes not covered at all. Always carry these items on board with you.

Although travelers are afraid of having their luggage lost, a report by the Department of Transportation shows that this only happens to about 5 in every 1,000 passengers. And, when it does happen, more than 50% of people get their bags back within 24 hours.

BUS & TRAIN

Think you'd rather leave the driving to someone else? Then you might want to consider taking a bus or train to school. Modern buses are big, plush, have bathrooms (loosely

defined), and sometimes even show movies. On the other hand, trains can be a bit more expensive than buses, but some people prefer the smooth ride, food service, and access to electrical outlets for items like a laptop.

These options may be less glamorous and slower than flying, but they are usually less expensive. Taking a bus or train should only take a little longer than driving if you can get direct transport. But depending on where you come from and where you're going, routes often end up either being very direct, or very inconvenient. Investigate your options using several different companies.

Cost

In general, taking the bus or train should leave you with more money in your pocket than some of your other options. Look for student rates to keep things even more low-budget. In choosing between the bus and the train, think about whether your trip will extend overnight. Trains often offer sleeper cars for a little more money. With a bus, you may need to fork out extra dough for a hotel if you can't sleep on board.

Luggage

Taking either a bus or a train will usually allow you to check more bags for less money than flying. Most bus lines permit two checked bags and two carry-ons. The bags you carry on have to fit under the seat or in the overhead compartment. If you need to check more than two bags, buses should allow you to do so. You can usually check a maximum of three additional pieces (for about $15 each). Buses will also let you bring a bike along for another $15. Each bag you check must weigh less than 60 pounds. One word of warning—the maximum liability most bus companies take is $250 for all of your baggage. Purchasing extra insurance may be smart if you're bringing a lot of stuff with you.

Most trains have limited room for carry-on baggage, so passengers are encouraged to check as much of their luggage as possible. Carry-on bags must weigh less than 50 pounds and fit under the seat or in the overhead compartment. In addition to carry-on bags, each ticketed passenger is allowed to check three bags weighing less than 50 pounds each. For an additional fee, most trains will allow you to check up to three additional bags or overweight items each weighing up to 75 pounds. You may also check special items such as bicycles, golf bags, musical instruments, or skis on trains, but again, there will be an additional fee. Most train carriers assume no responsibility for carry-on baggage and a maximum liability of $500 for each passenger's checked baggage. You will need to pay more to declare additional valuation which you can do for up to about $2,500.

DRIVING

Shhh... listen. That's the sound of the open road. Moving to college is a great road trip. It's also a way to take a lot of stuff to school. Share the adventure with a friend who is going to college in the same area, or spend some quality time on the road with your parents and little brother. Admit it: You're going to miss them once you're away at school.

Since you have to get to school in time for orientation, leave early and give yourself plenty of time to make the trip. If it's long drive, plan a few stops along the way to keep things interesting. If you always wanted to see Mt. Rushmore, Graceland, and Area 51, now's your chance. Whatever your destination, these tips will make getting there half the fun.

The Vehicle

Jack Kerouac left for his famous road trip with a canvas bag of necessities and $50 in his pocket. Chances are that everything you have isn't going to fit into a single canvas bag, but you probably won't have room for more than a carload of stuff in your dorm room. After you're done packing, you might not have space for Grandma to come along on the ride, but that's all right—you'll see her at Christmas.

If your car isn't roomy enough to carry all your earthly possessions, your parents, your little brother, and the stuff they brought along with them for the trip (You overpacked, didn't you?), rent a trailer, van, or truck. In most cases, how much you will spend on any of these options will depend on how far you are traveling for your move to campus, how long you will need the rented vehicle, and whether you need it for a one way or round trip.

Renting a trailer: If you just need to scare up a little more space, you may want to consider renting a trailer to make the trip with you. Available at most moving truck rental companies, trailers look like enclosed little carts that attach to the back of your car. Unless you're bringing a futon or some other large piece of furniture, it should give you all the space you need. However, there are a few drawbacks— your car must be a certain weight to haul one and able to have a trailer hitch attached. What's more, you can't drive faster than 45 mph with it in tow. (Luckily, Mount Rushmore looks good at that speed.)

Renting a cargo van or moving truck: The next step up from a trailer is to rent a cargo van, pickup truck, or 10-foot

TRAVEL TRAVAILS

I was about to start my freshman year at Boston College, and my mother and I were driving there one weekend so I could attend a special orientation. Earlier in the week I had avided my father's help with directions. His large collection of maps and atlases was daunting; furthermore, I saw this as a chance to show off my newly-acquired Internet skills. I decided to use a new website I had read about where I could enter my home address and my destination and, in seconds, receive a full set of directions right on the screen.

When the day of the trip arrived, we loaded up the station wagon and set out on the six-hour drive, thanking modern technology for the ease it provided. Aside from the countless tolls on the Garden State Parkway, it was a smooth trip and as we neared our destination, I read grandly from the directions, "Finally, take exit 17—the Newton/Watertown exit."

Relief soon turned to confusion. "Where is it?" We faced a Sheraton and a cluster of different shops. "The directions say get off at Exit 17," I said defensively. "Then what?" my mom asked. "I don't know, that's all it says!"

Over the next two hours, we thoroughly explored suburban Boston, but got no closer to school. Frustrated, I stared into the distance, pondering the blunders of modern technology. Suddenly I saw a tall Gothic tower above the trees.

"Wait, there it is!" Re-energized, I pointed out the tower. It was the same building pictured on the application booklet. We headed in its direction and eventually located the gates to the college. We were finally there, my home for the next four years, and I couldn't believe how we'd found it.

Looking back, I know problems always arise with traveling and I should have been prepared. I'm sure BC provided directions, and we should have taken one of my father's maps "just in case."

— Carey K., Boston College

moving truck. When considering this option, keep in mind that as soon as you are driving one of these rented vehicles and not your own car, your seating is reduced and you're no longer driving a vehicle to which you are accustomed. Regardless, you should have enough space with any of these three options. Rates vary dramatically depending on how far you're traveling and whether you plan to return the vehicle where you rented it, so you should call your local company to get rates and availability.

Renting a minivan or SUV: If you want more cargo space and a comfortable ride, you may want to consider renting a minivan or SUV. Call major car rental companies for prices. You'll get a reliable car with more space than your family's compact vehicle, but you'll still transport the whole family more comfortably than in a moving truck.

PLACES TO STAY

Depending on how far you'll be traveling to school, you may need to find a place to stay the night during your first trip. Knowing the best places to catch your 40 winks will come in handy for this first trip, as well as for the remainder of your college career. Undoubtedly, many situations will arise when you'll need to arrange for a place to stay: overnight stops traveling to and from school, spring break, weekend road trips, parents' weekend, and the times when your roommate and his or her "special friend" unexpectedly lock you out late at night, are just a few. In the latter situation, your next-door neighbor's futon will probably suffice. But for the other times, you'll need a different sort of accommodation.

Hotels

Hotels and motels are definitely the standard place to stay when you're on the road with your family or your parents visit you at school. If you stay in a hotel on your way to campus, ask about parking. Since you'll be traveling with all your belongings, you'll either need to leave them in your car if the parking area is secure, or haul everything into your room with you. For a place to stay when you get to campus, book a room at least two to three months in advance. Hotels in college towns go fast during peak times like move-in day, graduation, and parents' weekends. Call your school to ask if they can recommend a good place to stay. If you're lucky, they might have a block of rooms reserved (at a special rate) for visiting parents and new students.

Sleep on it:

According to U.S.News & World Report, the average price for a hotel room is $75 per night. Be prepared to pay more if you're staying in a big city or during peak travel periods.

Although the standard place to stay, hotels and motels are usually not cheap unless they're seedy. Remember this when you're making reservations for parents' weekend. Would you want your mom staying at a joint with Magic Fingers? If you're recommending a hotel near your campus to your parents, or making a reservation for them, go check it out ahead of time and make sure they'll find it both affordable and comfortable. If they don't, rest assured you'll hear about it.

When you're traveling with friends on a budget, it's okay to be a little less discerning. Pass up the four-star hotel with room service and a swimming pool every once in a while and consider it an adventure to stay in a roadside motel with blinking neon lights.

Staying in hotels can get a little pricey. Remember everything you learned about getting a good deal on airfare, because the same goes here: Reserve early. Be flexible. Ask for a student discount. In addition, here are some new tips:

Compare rates: Surfing the Internet can be the quickest and easiest way to find the best deals. Once you've found a hotel you're interested in online, call the hotel directly to see if you can get a better rate over the phone. Then call the national 800 number and check the rate with them. Each distributor may be offering a special that the other is not aware

of, so you may be able to get a better deal on the same exact room if you shop around. Also make sure to inquire about any special rates you might be eligible for as a student or member of an automobile club.

Share a room: Hotel rooms usually come with two full beds. Why not make the most of them? Most hotels allow up to four guests per room, so it makes sense to share a room when you are traveling with family or friends. Some people have tried to squeeze more than that in one room, but even if you think plush carpet is a close substitute for a firm mattress and that there's no real reason why 10 people can't share a room, consider that you may get caught. Be prepared to pay for enough rooms for everyone in your party. This is especially true during peak times like spring break when hotels are on the lookout for suspicious-looking college students trying to save a buck.

Consider the fringe benefits: Staying at a more expensive hotel might provide a cheaper vacation than staying at a cheaper hotel if you look at the entire package. Will the expensive but conveniently-located hotel save you a dozen cab fares downtown? Will it eliminate the need for a rental car? Does it include breakfast? Or a kitchen? Before booking at a cheap hotel, add up the extra benefits of a more expensive hotel to make sure it's not actually a better deal.

If you don't have a reservation: Don't just show up on the doorstep of a hotel looking like a lost puppy if you don't have a reservation. If you are already inside the hotel, the clerk knows you're not likely to leave, so you probably won't be offered the best rate. Instead, if you call ahead you will have a better chance at getting the cheapest rate. The hotel knows it is easy for you to keep shopping around when you're already on the phone, so they'll probably just quote you their lowest rate right off the bat.

Youth Hostels

Rooms in hostels, unlike those in hotels, are usually furnished with bunk beds and shared with other guests. Sharing facilities creates a congenial atmosphere and keeps the cost down, so you'll only have to pay about $10 to $25 per night. You should be able to find an inexpensive, clean hostel in most cities around the world. However, hostels are probably a better option when you're traveling alone or with friends rather than with your family. To find a hostel in an area you'll be visiting, check online or buy a directory from a bookstore.

Camping

When your destination is far from civilization, camping may be your best (or only) bet. Camping is a fun and cheap alternative to other accommodations. If you already own essentials like a tent and sleeping bag, you'll only have to pay about $5 to $10 a night for a camp site. Just don't forget a flashlight and a bottle of bug spray!

HOLIDAYS & BREAKS

Amazing as it sounds, you need to start thinking about your holidays and breaks well ahead of time, possibly even before you get to school! As a student you are virtually guaranteed to be traveling on all the busiest days of the year, like Thanksgiving and New Year's, just when it's hardest to get a good airline ticket or bus seat. Also, Thanksgiving isn't that far away from the beginning of the school year. When you're making airline reservations for your trip to school, you may want to make plans ahead of time to use the return trip on that ticket to get home for the holiday or winter break.

If you're planning ahead for any flights that would come after final exams, you probably won't know when your last final is until very late in the term. Look on your school's website for an academic calendar or call your school for the date of the last day of finals. Book your ticket for the evening of the last day of exams if you want to be on the safe side. The alternative would be to negotiate to take an exam ahead of time if you book your flight too early. Some professors may be reasonable enough to let you do this, but if yours refused, you'd have to pay a fee to change your ticket home.

One of the most legendary college experiences is, of course, spring break. Not long after you arrive on campus, you'll start to see advertisements. Even if it feels early to be thinking about spring break, many of the best packages fill up ahead of time. Keep an eye out. Knowing what's out there will also help you budget. Once you get an idea how much your dream trip may cost, you can start saving up (or rethinking your plans!).

Bon Voyage!

FuturePages, a college media agency, surveyed college students and found that 60% of them travel for vacation purposes each year. And to figure out where to jet off to next—almost 70% of students research potential travel destinations online.

For those able to travel, spring break is certainly the perfect antidote to the pressures of classes, homework, and midterms. Every year, students from all across the country head south—flocking everywhere from Florida to Mexico to the Caribbean in search of sun, fun, and parties all night long. If this is what you're looking for, you won't be disappointed. But if this isn't your idea of a dream vacation, there are thousands of other packages available to students. Some involve exploring the streets of a European village, while others offer opportunities to volunteer in the inner city. There's something great out there, no matter what your interests, so be persistent.

As you've already learned, most vacations will come cheap and convenient if you go through a travel agent or student travel service that offers package deals. Starting in the fall, these companies won't be hard to come by. In fact, they'll practically find you. Just read the message boards in your residence hall, cafeteria, or student union and you'll see hundreds of travel companies competing for your business. Some of them are legitimate—others are not. Find out exactly what the vacation package you're considering includes. Many tour companies include hotel, airfare, and meals in their vacation packages. Sometimes, things sound too good to be true—and are. Be sure to check out the supplier, tour operator, or travel agent with The Council of Better Business Bureaus (www.bbb.org) before you book your trip.

PART THREE

PERSONAL
FINANCE

BANKING

You've worked hard at your part-time job and amassed a small fortune to bring to college. Stuffing those bills under your mattress would be easy, yes, but it's definitely not your best option. What would prevent an evil roommate from pilfering the money while you're not looking? The best place to stash your money is a bank—and not just because they'll keep it safe.

Opening a bank account is a smart move: It provides you with a place to keep your money, helps you earn interest on your funds, and gives you a way to pay your bills. Even if you didn't need a checking account in high school, in college you definitely will. The pizza delivery guy might take cash, but the phone company won't.

To conduct all your business and keep your money under lock and key, you'll want at least a checking account and probably a savings account, too. A third option is a money market account, but they're not as useful for the average college student since they tend to require much higher minimum balances and pay only nominally higher interest rates on your money.

Opening a checking account gives you easy access to a portion of your money for day-to-day expenses and bill paying, while opening a savings account will earn you interest on the majority of your funds. Putting your money in the two separate accounts also helps some students budget their money. You can keep this month's money in checking, and let the rest of your funds stay in savings. If you realize a check you wrote is about to bounce, transferring money from one account to another is easy to do over the phone, at an ATM, or online.

This chapter will tell you what you need to know about setting up a bank account at school and using it wisely.

FINDING A BANK

If you already have a bank account in your hometown, the first thing you should do is find out if they have a branch or ATM near your college. If they do, consider yourself lucky—you can keep your account with them. This will allow you easy access to your funds while you're at school or at home during breaks.

If your hometown bank does not have an office or ATM near campus, open new accounts with a bank at school. Keeping your old bank exclusively would mean paying ATM fees through the nose—not to mention the extreme inconvenience of having to mail all of your deposits to your bank and then waiting for them to clear so you could use the money.

If you need to open an account with a new bank, check out your choices by searching online, checking with the area Chamber of Commerce (try www.chamberofcommerce.com), asking people at school, or walking around town during an early trip to campus.

Contact a few of the nearby banks to find out what they offer. You can usually get this information by visiting websites or getting copies of their promotional pamphlets through one of their branch offices, either in person or by calling to request information. Whenever talking with banks, be sure to ask if they offer student packages. Such packages, publicized or not, usually offer lower monthly fees, lower ATM fees, and other perks. When investigating banks, here's what to look for:

Size Matters

Although a bank's size in itself will probably not make you decide to use it, its size can be an indicator of what to expect. Generally, smaller banks tend to be local and some say more student-friendly; because these banks are smaller, the business they receive from college students will probably be more important to them than it is to a larger bank, so the service is likely to be better, too. On the flip side, larger interstate banks have more resources, resulting in more extras: more locations (especially when you go out of town, since these banks operate in more than one state), more ATMs, and added features like online banking. In some cases, the trade-off for these extras is decreased personal service and higher fees.

Location, Location, Location

In selecting a bank, part of what you're looking for is convenience. A large part of what makes a bank convenient (or inconvenient) is its location and the location of its ATMs.

The savings will add up every term if you choose a bank close by with enough ATMs so you won't be tempted to use one belonging to another bank.

Rates And Fees

At the heart of your banking decision are interest rates and fees. There shouldn't be a big difference between the rates competing banks will pay you on the money you keep with them. In contrast, fees can vary widely. Since it's unlikely that the amount of money in your account will make you rich in interest, it's most important to find a bank that won't make you poor with fees. Pay attention to the three basic fees banks charge:

Monthly fees: The amount the bank will charge you each month just to have an account.

Transaction fees: The additional charges you pay each time you use an ATM or write a check more often than you are allowed or use another bank's ATM.

Penalties: The fees you are charged for violating certain restrictions—for example, if you bounce a check.

To put these fees into actual numbers, if you sign up for a checking account with a $10 monthly fee, use another bank's ATM once per month, and bounce just one check—not an unreasonable assumption—over the course of a year, your bank account will cost you about $175!

SELECTING AN ACCOUNT

Now that you have seen how quickly fees can add up, you'll understand why it's important to choose your account wisely. It's not the bank that gives out the coolest T-shirts during orientation that should get your account—it's the one that offers you the best banking value (or at least the lowest fees!). Here are some tips to help you minimize the fees you'll have to pay:

Master The Minimum Balance

Usually the only way to avoid paying a monthly fee is to maintain a minimum balance in your account. But the question is: Will you always have at least $1,000 in the bank? How about $2,500? Those are the minimum balances many banks require. If you sign up for an account with a minimum balance requirement, you'll want to play it safe:

Keep it up: Make sure you can maintain your minimum, not just in September when you're flush with cash from your summer job, but all year long. If you dip below the minimum, you will be charged. Sometimes this charge will be more than if you had signed up for an account without a balance requirement, since your account probably came with extra features and fewer restrictions.

Know your methods: Look for a bank that uses an average daily balance method for calculating your account balance. With this method, as long as your average balance over the month exceeds the minimum, you won't have to pay a fee. Banks that use a daily balance method will charge you if your account dips below the minimum balance requirement on any day during the month.

Shrink The Monthly Fee

Unless you've got the bucks for a minimum balance, chances are you won't escape paying a monthly fee. But if you're savvy you can reduce it by following these tips:

Shop around: The monthly fee will vary between banks, so compare and flash your student ID in case it can save you a couple of bucks.

Direct deposit: If you have a part-time job, some banks will waive monthly fees if you have your check deposited directly into your account by your employer.

Skimp: Consider asking for a no-frills or lifeline checking account if you won't have a lot of transactions each month. Offered by some banks and required by law in some states, these accounts offer reduced checking benefits at reduced rates; you only get to write 8-10 checks per month before being hit with extra charges, but your monthly fee is usually under $5.

Go away: Don't take it personally, but some banks will offer you a really low monthly fee if they never have to see you again. Essentially, in exchange for the lower fee, you're agreeing to do all banking by ATM, over the phone, or online. This saves the bank money because they don't have to employ as many people, but it also means that if you ever need to talk to someone with a question that can't be answered by an automatic system, you'll be charged for it.

Think small: If you're striking out with big banks, sometimes smaller banks will charge less either because they offer fewer extras or because they are trying to compete with the big guys.

Avoid ATM Fees

On your way to meet friends for dinner, you realize you don't have enough cash on you. Fortunately, you see an ATM down the block and stop to get money. Unfortunately, the ATM belongs to another bank. They charge you a fee, your bank charges you a fee, and all of a sudden it costs you $3 to take out $20. ATM fees like that can add up quickly, and so can other transaction fees. To minimize what you'll pay:

Play by the rules: Is your account limited to 10 checks per month? Five ATM transactions? Stay within these guidelines to avoid fees. Also know what counts as a transaction: Just withdrawals? Deposits? Account inquiries?

Don't stray: Use your own bank's ATM as often as possible. Know what your bank charges if you use another bank's ATM. And know what the other bank will charge you, too.

Once you've done all your homework and you know what account you want to open and where you want to open it, the real fun begins. If possible, open your new account before you move to campus. Opening your account early will give you access to your money as soon as you arrive. You'll appreciate the head start, since you'll need money right away for lots of things like tuition, activity fees, and textbooks.

Once you know which account you want, most banks will let you open it over the phone or on a website. The bank will need your Social Security Number, an ID such as a copy of your driver's license or other state-issued card, and sufficient funds to open the account, usually in the form of a check. At some point, you may also be asked to sign a signature card for the bank to use when verifying your transactions. Lastly, if you're signing up for a special student package, you'll most likely need a copy of your student ID.

If you don't get a chance to open your account before you move, you may be inconvenienced, but you'll survive. Banks often set up tables during orientation so new students can open accounts. By applying this way, you might even get a free T-shirt or coffee mug out of the deal. But don't forget what you've just learned: Choose your bank by its accounts, not the free gifts.

ACCESSING YOUR FUNDS

So, you've signed up with a bank and given them your wads of cash from the summer. Now what? How are you going to use that money to pay for stuff?

Checks

When you first open your account, your bank will give you starter checks. There are just a few of these, and you'll have to write your address on them yourself, but they'll get you by the first couple of days.

BANKING BLUNDER

In high school I was one of those kids who stuffed all my money into a secret desk drawer, not the bank. Until I packed up my things and went to Tufts, my rumpled balls of $1 and $5 bills co-existed quite happily with old birthday cards and chewed-up pencils.

In college I learned that getting a bank account is easy. It's navigating the rules and keeping up-to-date on your account that's difficult. Before moving to campus, I signed up for an account with a prominent Boston bank. Since I knew I'd be moving a lot over the next four years, I used my parents' address as the home address on the account. It seemed like the easiest thing to do, but in retrospect, it made keeping up with my account more difficult. My monthly bank statements were sent to my parents' house and then my mother would mail them to me. I almost never read them because I didn't think they were important.

Eventually, I was so behind that I didn't realize my bank was merging with a much larger bank. I also failed to understand the implications this had for my little student checking account. One afternoon I was in the campus center using the ATM, and those nine dreaded words appeared on the screen: YOUR ACCOUNT HAS INSUFFICIENT FUNDS TO COMPLETE THIS TRANSACTION. My heart pounded and I blushed bright red. How could this have happened?

As it turned out, my new, bigger bank wasn't as kind to students as my old bank had been. There were significant penalties for not maintaining a minimum balance, plus other checking account fees and penalties. All these charges had added up and now, instead of having money in the bank, I owed money to the bank!

I'd be lying if I said this only happened once, but I eventually got my act together. I started keeping tabs on my account balance and figured out my bank's fees. In the end I learned you don't have to be a financial whiz to avoid paying the bank a ton of money. You just have to pay attention.

— Cloe A., Tufts University

Your bank may also provide free checks printed with your name and address on them. If not, you can get them yourself by ordering from your bank, or through one of the many companies that advertise in the coupon section of the newspaper. You don't really need to order too many checks at once. You probably won't be writing all that many, and since most merchants require them to be printed with your local address, don't get more than you'll use before you change dorm rooms—and possibly mailing addresses.

If you tend to be absent-minded or disorganized, you should consider duplicate checks. With duplicates, you get a carbon copy of each check you write, in case you forget to log it in your account register.

It will take a while for any checks you've written to be deducted from your balance. The time in between check-writing and deduction is called "float." The same period occurs when you deposit a check. Depending on what kind of check it is (payroll, personal, etc.) and what bank it's from (in-state or out-of-state) the funds will be available at varying times. See the sidebar to learn more about float.

The Check Register

The check register is the lined booklet and calendar you get along with your checks to keep track of how much money you have. Make sure every transaction you make is recorded in your register. This includes any checks, any deposits or withdrawals at the ATM, or any electronic purchases you make with a debit or check card. At the end of the month, compare your register with your bank statement. If you find errors, double-check your work and then contact the bank and have them correct it. Doing this each month will help you be sure that however much money you think you have in your account, your bank agrees.

If you don't keep track of your account in your check register, or unfortunately maybe even if you do, you may bounce a check. This is when you write a check, but don't have enough money in your account to cover it. According to a survey by Quicken, makers of personal finance software, almost 50% of students do this at least once during college. This is something you should strive to avoid, because it will cost you—your bank will charge you up to $25 dollars, and whomever you wrote the check to can charge you another $25.

To prevent bouncing, not only watch your check register carefully, but also consider getting overdraft protection. With this feature, if you write a check you can't cover, the bank will still cover it so that it won't bounce. The check will be paid and then you will owe the bank whatever amount you were short, plus interest. If you're interested in signing up for this, ask your bank. Normally, you have to apply for this separately because it's a form of credit.

According to The Wall Street Journal's *Guide to Understanding Personal Finance*, the rules of float are as follows: If you deposit a government, certified, bank, or travelers check it should clear in one day, as should an electronic transfer. If you deposit a check for $100 which was written on a local bank, you should be able to withdraw $10 of the $100 one day later, $40 on the second day, and the remaining $50 on the third day. On an out-of-town check, you can withdraw $10 one day later and the other $90 five days later.

ATM, Debit Cards, And Check Cards

Depending on where you bank, you have a few options for making electronic inquiries or transactions with your bank account:

ATM card: This is the basic card that you should absolutely get with your account. You use this card at an ATM to make balance inquiries and deposit, withdraw, and transfer money. Inserting your card in a little slot prompts the ATM to ask you for your Personal Identification Number (PIN). When you enter the correct PIN, the ATM will process your transaction (provided that you have enough funds in your account to do so).

When you open your account, the bank representative will ask you to select your PIN. Your PIN should be a combination of at least four numbers that only you know. Do not choose your birth date, Social Security number, or any other obvious number. Most importantly, do not tell anyone what your PIN is or write it down in your wallet. (That is, unless you want someone to steal all your money.)

Check card: Check cards look like ATM cards, but they carry the Visa or MasterCard logo and you can't use them at ATMs because they don't require a PIN. Instead, you use this

card wherever Visa or MasterCard is accepted and sign a receipt, much as you would if paying by credit card. Funds will usually be deducted from your account within two to three days, but not immediately. Normally, you have this card in addition to your ATM card, or you have a...

Debit card: Debit cards combine the function of the ATM card and the check card in one shiny little piece of plastic. This card will carry the Visa or MasterCard logo, but it will also have a PIN number so you can use it at ATMs. When using it to make a transaction, you can usually choose to use it like an ATM card, entering a PIN and having the funds immediately removed from your account, or like a check card, where you sign a receipt and the funds are deducted a few days later.

It's important that before using any of these cards you:

- Understand the fees involved for doing so. Many times a bank will charge you if you exceed a certain number of transactions in a given month.

- Remember to record the transaction in your check register.

- Keep your receipt, not only so you don't forget to record the transaction, but also because they often contain personal information about your account.

- Don't lose your card or go to the ATM alone at night. Safety first!

Online Banking

Yet another option that has become very popular is online banking, which allows you to view and make transactions using your accounts over the Internet. Not only can you make these transactions 24 hours a day, like at an ATM, but you can do it from the comfort and safety of your own dorm room.

Another benefit of online banking is that it allows you to pay your bills online or even set up recurring automatic payments for regular bills such as rent. This means no more checks to write, due dates to remember, or envelopes to lick. Not all banks offer online banking and many charge extra for it (sometimes quite a bit), so before you register, make sure it's a feature you will use. If you don't have a lot of bills to pay or are just going to use it to check your balance, it's probably not worth it. Get off your lazy butt and walk to an ATM!

CHAPTER EIGHT

CREDIT CARDS

In addition to opening your new bank account, consider signing up for a credit card. A credit card is basically a convenient way to pay for something using borrowed money. If you go to a store and pay using a credit card, you leave without turning over a cent. Your credit card company pays the store and then you pay the credit card company at the end of the month. From the time you leave the store to when you pay your credit card bill, you're borrowing money and using credit.

Credit cards get a bad rap because a lot of people don't use them responsibly; they get into financial trouble by using them to buy products they can't afford and not paying their bills. But for responsible consumers, credit cards are convenient to have and sometimes downright necessary. Just a few reasons you'd want a card:

- You anticipate having school-related expenses for which you need a credit card—for example, your loan money won't be sent until October, but you need to buy books in August.

- You need to make purchases over the phone or online.

- You commute to school and want to be safe in case of emergency (flat tire, stranded during a snow storm, etc.).

- You want to build a good credit history by responsibly paying your bills. Then, when you need to borrow larger amounts of money later in life (for a car or house), you'll have shown you're trustworthy.

This chapter will teach you what to look for in your first card, the ins and outs of applying for credit, and tips for using your credit responsibly.

CREDIT 101

Before jumping on the credit card bandwagon, you'll want to make sure you understand how credit works. The worst thing you can do is spend now and figure it out later. As long as you get a card knowing what it's for (paying for things you can afford) and what it's not for (pizza for the entire dorm, $200 pairs of shoes, calls to the psychic network) you're halfway there. To figure the rest out, keep reading and learn the basics that everyone using credit should know.

Types Of Cards

There are two basic types of credit cards: store cards, only good for purchases at the particular retailer who issued the

CREDIT TO THE RESCUE

I never realized how important it was to have a credit card in an emergency until I found myself in one. Traveling with friends during my sophomore year, I found myself in a strange city without a place to stay. The only thing that saved me and my friends from having to sleep on the streets on a crowded and unruly Halloween weekend was my emergency credit card.

When we first arrived in Amsterdam we felt very prepared, because everything was just as the guidebooks said it would be. But, although the guidebooks also said the city had plenty of lodging, as we started walking around the city, peeping into hostels, they all seemed very full. When we finally found a hostel that wasn't packed and seemed OK, we went in, paid for our beds, and took off for our day of sightseeing.

Around midnight we returned to our hostel to find a co-ed dormitory-style room with an unfortunate odor, a naked man sleeping in my friend's bed and bathrooms that didn't lock. We couldn't stay there, so after fighting unsuccessfully to get our money back, we were out in the cold, on Halloween, at 1:30 a.m.

We traipsed around the city looking for somewhere to stay, but everywhere was closed or full. Then we found our last beacon of hope: the five-star Victoria Hotel. The man at the front desk said they also had no vacancies, not a room, not a broom closet, nothing. Then miraculously, as we stood there considering our options, the clerk found a reservation that had expired at midnight. The room was available and had plenty of space for four weary travelers, but it was the penthouse suite and no, there wasn't a student discount.

Even after pooling our cash we didn't have enough money for the room, but luckily, I had my emergency credit card! Certain my parents would agree this qualified as an emergency, I handed it to the clerk. We were safe! I was thankful that my parents had insisted I carry a credit card with me, just in case.

— Mara H., Binghamton University

card (Sears, Exxon, Macy's, etc.), and universal cards, good for purchases of almost anything anywhere (Visa, MasterCard, American Express, Discover). It's probably best to make your first card a universal card.

The brand of universal card you choose usually matters less than the terms set by the company that issues it. For instance, whether your card has a MasterCard or a Visa logo on it, the card will be accepted nearly everywhere. You should be more concerned about whether the card charges a $50 annual fee.

Paying off a $1,000 credit card balance in $15 minimum monthly payments would take you five years, and with an interest rate of 16%, would cost you about $450 in interest. Yikes!

Terms Of Credit

The terms of credit defined by your credit card company will cover many things, including:

Credit limit: Your credit limit is the predetermined amount of money your credit card issuer agrees to lend you. You will not be allowed to spend more than this, but your limit will increase over time as you use your card responsibly. Since you're a student, your credit limit may start out fairly low, possibly as low as $100.

Annual fee: Some issuers charge once-a-year fees for simply having a credit card. The fees are generally in the vicinity of $50 to $100, and they're most common with cards issued to people with bad credit, or with cards that carry rewards programs.

Interest rate: The interest rate on your card determines how much you'll pay in finance charges if you don't pay your bill in full each month. Interest rates are stated in terms of an APR, or Annual Percentage Rate. Get the card with the lowest rate possible.

Minimum payment: The minimum payment is the least

amount of money your credit card company will accept at the end of the month to consider your account in good standing. Usually this is somewhere between $10 and $50, depending on your balance. Always pay more than this amount—if not your entire balance—each month, and never accept offers to lower your minimum payment or skip a payment. This will only delay the inevitable and result in higher finance charges—you have to pay the bill off eventually.

Late fees: You'll be charged a late fee if you don't make at least your minimum payment before your due date. Although many credit card companies will give you a cushion of a few days before they penalize you, you don't want to take your chances. Late fees can be steep, often as high as $30. Pay your bill on time to avoid these fees and keep your credit in good shape!

Rewards programs: Many credit cards offer incentives such as frequent flyer miles or cash back on purchases. While these bonuses are great, these cards usually have disadvantages like an annual fee or high APR.

The Right Card For You

Beyond understanding the terms set by card issuers, choosing a credit card is all about how you'll be using it. Certainly you want to strive to pay your entire bill each month, which means you're not spending more than you can afford, but be realistic about it. Ask yourself if you will be able to pay off your entire bill each month, or if it's more likely that you will carry a balance from month to month. Then choose a card based on your answer.

If you will pay in full each month: Congratulations! If you are the type of person to pay your balance in full each month, interest rates won't matter much to you. Instead, look for a card with:

- No annual fee.

- A grace period. Most cards will offer them, but make sure you get a grace period on all your purchases. This is the number of days before you are charged interest on your balance. The average grace period is 25 days.

- A rewards program. Cards that offer rewards usually come with higher interest rates, so they don't make sense for people who carry a balance, but for someone like you, they might be perfect. Don't expect to make out like a bandit, but at least it's something for your money—some cards will give you a percentage of your purchases back in cash, say $1 or $2 on every $100 you spend. Others will give you free airline tickets or points you can use towards gifts.

If you will carry a balance: If you think you might not pay your bill off each month, you'll want a card that lets you minimize the amount you have to pay in finance charges to the credit card company. Look for a card with:

- No annual fee.

- Low interest rate. Since you are a student with only a limited credit history, it may be difficult for you to get a low rate. But as you build a good credit history by paying your bill on time, ask your credit card company for a better rate, or shop around for another card.

- Look for a card that calculates finance charges using the average daily balance method as opposed to the two-cycle billing method. Basically, under the daily balance method your finance charge will be based on the sum of money you owe at the end of each day over a one-month period, divided by the number of days in the month and then multiplied by your monthly periodic interest rate (your APR divided by 12).

- Pay your bill as soon as you get it. When you carry a balance, you forfeit your grace period. You are charged interest on the balance you carry forward into the month, and you are also immediately charged interest on all your new purchases.

- Always pay more than the minimum and as much as you can.

OBTAINING AND USING CREDIT

Now that you know how credit works and what kind of card is right for you, you're ready to apply for your first card!

Finding Credit Card Offers

Say you want to find a universal credit card that you can use to pay for books, clothes, and airline tickets, as well as have on hand in case of emergency. Where do you look? Advertisements for credit cards are prevalent and can be found online, through direct mail, postered on walls at school, in newspapers, and even in the pages of this book. In searching for a card, concentrate on offers for student cards. They're the most likely to accept people who have limited to no credit history.

Applying For Credit

Once you find a credit card offer you like, you need to fill out the application to get it. Each application is a little different, but they all require information such as your name, birth date, address (possibly your permanent address at home in addition to your school address), Social Security Number, and information about your income (term-time wages plus any allowance your parents may give you). It's important that you keep the information on these applications private—don't fill one out and leave it lying in your dorm room!

Start Building Good Credit For A Great Future.

Apply For Your Student Card Today!*

Now with online account access! Get up-to-the-minute account information, schedule electronic payments, review recent statements and much more.

Please mention priority code SAC8

1-866-GET-MBNA

TTY Users, please call 1-800-833-6262

After you apply for a card, the credit card company requests a copy of your credit report. Your credit report is based on your name, address, and Social Security Number and tells the creditor your credit history. The creditor will see if you have any debts, and every time over the past seven years that you've applied for a loan, requested a credit card, or been denied credit.

If you wish to check out your credit reports in advance, call the three credit bureaus for copies or have a third party or service do so for you. The three credit bureaus are are Experian Consumer Assistance, Equifax, and Trans Union.

Chances are your credit report will contain very little information, since you probably haven't applied for any serious loans outside of your financial aid. A blank credit history is both a good and bad thing. It will probably make it easy to get approved for a card, since you have no strikes against you, but as we mentioned, you'll likely start out with a low credit limit and a moderately-high APR.

If your credit card application is denied because of bad credit history, you can still try for a secured card. Think of a secured card as a bike with training wheels. You basically deposit money in a special savings account as collateral with the bank that issues you the card. Charges you make then go against this amount, in case you do not pay. After using a secured card responsibly, you will be able to graduate to a traditional credit card.

Playing It Smart

As soon as you get your credit card in the mail, sign the back and call the 800 number stuck to the card to activate it. Then, make a photocopy of the front and back of your

card and store it someplace safe, along with any papers you received with the card.

If you ever lose your card or it's stolen, you'll want to use this information to call your credit card company immediately. This will allow them to stop anyone else from using your card and get you a new one. If you're not quick enough and someone does make an unauthorized purchase using

your credit card, federal law limits your liability for credit card fraud at $50. However, most credit card companies waive this fee entirely.

Make sure you keep all your credit card receipts in your wallet or in an envelope during the month. Then when you receive your bill, you can compare your statement to your saved receipts and make sure that there are no discrepancies. If there are unexpected charges, call your credit card company immediately to file a dispute. Your credit card company will most likely freeze the amount you're disputing, so you won't be expected to pay it until they have investigated the transaction.

Keeping track of what you're charging will also help you to spend less. When you start having trouble closing your wallet because you have so many receipts in there, you know it's time to stop spending. If you find that this is not enough, try keeping a running tally with each receipt you add to your wallet or envelope each month. Or check with your credit card company online or by phone to find out your interim balance. This is the best way not to be surprised at the end of the month that you can't pay your bill.

Be wary of taking cash advances. If you use your credit card to get a cash advance, you will be charged a transaction fee equal to some percentage of your withdrawal. You'll also be charged interest on that money right away (cash advances never get a grace period) and it's usually a higher rate than you pay on your regular purchases. Beware: If you get blank checks in the mail from your credit card company, they are cash advances in disguise.

If you ever find yourself in an emergency situation and don't have the money to pay off your entire bill at the end of the month, don't panic, but pay as much as you can. Just be sure to catch up during the next month. You should never just ignore your bill, skip a month's payment, or send in a check that you "forget" to sign or don't have the money to cover. Credit card companies have seen it all and pulling stunts usually results in more fees and finance charges. If you don't have the money to pay your bill, contact the credit card company immediately and try to work it out with them. Generally, as long as you are making an effort to pay off your balance, they'll understand; they would prefer to get a small payment than no payment at all.

CHAPTER NINE

INSURANCE

What do you do when your dorm has been burglarized and your laptop stolen, or when you've been in a car accident and there's a big dent in your front end? You have insurance.

Whether you'll continue on your parents' insurance policies or get one of your own, it's important to make sure you're covered in case of emergency. Having good health and dental insurance, either through your parents or through your school, will keep you healthy and smiling pretty. Property insurance on the contents of your dorm room and insurance on your car, if you bring one to school, will keep you from going broke in case of theft, fire, or other disaster.

This chapter helps you sort out which kinds of insurance you may need, including renter's, car, and health insurance, and shares tips for finding affordable coverage. But before you dive into specific types of insurance you may need, here are some basic facts:

What It's Good For

Insurance protects you from the unexpected and unfortunate. You pay the insurance company small amounts called premiums so when disaster strikes (and it will), you don't have to pay a lot all at once. You might pay $100 a year to insure your dorm room, but if the sprinklers go off and everything in your room is destroyed, you don't have to pay $5,000 to replace it all. Your insurance company will pay for everything, minus your deductible (the fixed amount you agree to pay before your insurance kicks in).

How To Get It

As a student, there's a good chance that you will get your insurance—especially health insurance—through your parents, but not necessarily. In general, people get their insurance in a few different ways: They buy insurance from an independent agent who sells the policies of different insurance companies, from a captive agent who only sells the policies of one particular company, directly from an insurance provider, or through a group to which they belong, such as an employer or in the case of students, a college.

Ways To Save

Although insurance may feel expensive when you're paying the premium each month, it's nothing compared to what you would have to pay if something bad happened. Still, there are two simple ways you can save: First, increase your deductible if you want to save on your premiums—just don't make it so high that you can't afford it if something happens. Second, shop around. In pricing your policy, insurance companies are betting on how much you'll cost them: How likely it is that something bad will happen to you and how much it will cost them if it does. Since this is some pretty complicated guesswork, premiums can vary widely from company to company. Get quotes from multiple insurance companies to get the best deal.

RENTER'S INSURANCE

Just because there is a feeling of community at college doesn't mean you should take your safety for granted. Unfortunately, things still happen, even on the most idyllic campuses. In fact, according to the Chronicle of Higher Education, burglary is the most frequently reported criminal incident on college campuses, with thousands of property crimes occurring each year. In addition to theft, there are other ways your belongings could be damaged, including fire or water.

While you may not think you have a lot of stuff, just imagine having to buy it all over again. Not so fun, right? Then get the insurance company to do it by making sure your belongings are covered by your parents' homeowner's policy or by your own renter's insurance.

On Your Parents' Policy

If your parents have a homeowner's insurance policy, the first thing you'll want to do is check with their insurance agent to see if your belongings will be insured when you go to school. Make sure their agent knows where you are going to school and where you will be living. Some insurance companies will be unable to insure you if your college is not in the same state as your parents' home. For others, that's not a problem. Similarly, some companies will require that you live in college housing in order to be covered, while others will cover your belongings even if you live off campus, as long as it's not considered your permanent address.

Students who are covered by their parents' homeowner's policy generally have their belongings covered for up to

ROBBED!

At the end of my freshman year, I packed up some of my belongings but left most of my stuff at school. My roommate and I were subletting our apartment for the summer and since we were moving back in the fall, we decided to leave most of our stuff for the tenants to use. We left our TVs, stereos, couch, and beds—pretty much everything.

At the end of the summer I checked in on things. Our tenants had locked the apartment and given their keys to the landlord. He was having some new carpet installed in the apartment, but it would all be done before I returned. This was great news!

Unfortunately, this excitement was short-lived. When I returned to the apartment to start fall term I saw a bunch of my stuff destroyed on the front lawn. Upon further investigation, I found our door unlocked and the rest of our possessions stolen.

I was outraged and immediately called the landlord. It turned out that he had called cleaners for the apartment next door and they had "mistakenly" thought that our apartment was to be cleaned out as well. They thought everything in the apartment was to be thrown out, including our stereos, TVs, posters, silverware, couches, and even our beds! They took anything they wanted and threw the rest of it on the lawn as garbage.

The landlord played dumb and claimed our lease specified that it was not his responsibility if anything was stolen. He said we should check our renter's insurance. Instead, we checked with a lawyer who said that since the landlord was responsible for the cleaners, he was also responsible for the theft.

In the end, we made a list of everything that was stolen or destroyed and got a check from our landlord's insurance company to replace everything. It was a hassle, but we were very lucky to get our stuff replaced. If it hadn't been covered by our landlord's insurance, we would probably still be sleeping on the floor and eating with our fingers in front of our "invisible" TV. It's really important to make sure your stuff is covered by insurance, no matter what!

— Rob N., Indiana University

10% of the parents' policy. For instance, if your parents have $100,000 in homeowner's insurance, their policy would cover $10,000 of your stuff. That's probably enough coverage for the average student, but you'll want to make sure that all the items you're bringing with you are covered under the policy. Prepare an inventory of your belongings and the approximate cost of replacing them. Use this list to verify with the agent that all of your larger ticket items will be covered. In some cases, items like jewelry, computers, or other electronics will not be covered under your parents' policy and you may want to consider purchasing an additional policy to cover them.

On Your Own

If you are not covered under your parents' policy or they don't have one, think about renter's insurance. It's important for your stuff to be insured, but if you're worried about how

much it will cost, there are some insurance companies that will allow you to share a policy with your roommate if he or she needs coverage, too. These policies are usually quite affordable, charging premiums around $150-$200 per year for coverage on both roommates' belongings, up to about $15,000 in property. It also helps to put things in perspective: That $100 you'll pay for insurance wouldn't even pay to replace your clothes if something happened to your dorm room. Not to mention your computer, stereo, bedding, and furniture.

Some insurance companies specialize in student property insurance, offering broader coverage than your parents' policy, with lower deductibles and premiums—be on the lookout for this student-tailored insurance that can save you grief.

CSI Student Personal Property Protector Plus℠

Replacement cost coverage for student property – for less than the cost of a homeowner's deductible

Fireman's Fund®

Property Insurance Designed For Students Living Away From Home

If you live in a residence hall or dorm, fraternity or sorority, or in off-campus apartments or rooms, you may not have proper protection from your parents' homeowner's policy.

Even with a homeowners policy, this is primary coverage. The Student Personal Property Protector Plus℠ plan is designed exclusively for students. It covers things a homeowner's policy does not. And our rates are affordable for student budgets.

Consider your options

There are three things to consider when ordering your CSI Student Personal Property Protector Plus.℠

1. How much insurance do you need?

Most people are amazed at how much they own. Use the Personal Property Inventory to estimate the value of your possessions. That total cost is the amount of insurance you should buy. We also think it's wise to add $1,000 to your total to accommodate things you may acquire.

2. What is the difference between Replacement Value and Actual Cash Value?

Replacement Value is the best choice for most students. If you have a total loss of an item, your policy will pay you for a new item of like quality for each of the items lost, no matter how old they are.

Actual Cash Value insurance means that you will recover the depreciated value of the items lost. This will be less than the new cost of the item. For many students this could be sufficient.

3. What is the deductible?

If you had a loss of $1,000 on a policy with a $50 deductible, you would receive your $1000 less the $50 for an actual payment of $950. Deductibles help lower the overall cost of your insurance. We offer three choices for your deductible.

The CSI guarantee means no risk to you

CSI guarantees that you will be happy with your coverage and backs it with a 30-day full refund, no questions asked guarantee. If you are not happy with your policy for any reason, just return it to us, marked "Cancel" and we will immediately refund your payment in full.

Should you wish to cancel at any later date, simply return the policy for a pro rata refund subject to a $45.00 minimum charge. We may cancel this policy by notifying you in writing.

Insure your student personal property today.

Use this chart to find your own annual premium.

Insurance Amount	Deductible	Actual Cash Value Annual Premium	Replacement Value Premium
$2,000	$25	$36	$50
	$50	$31	$43
	$100	$26	$36
$3,000	$25	$54	$76
	$50	$49	$69
	$100	$44	$62
$4,000	$25	$72	$101
	$50	$67	$94
	$100	$62	$87
$5,000	$25	$90	$126
	$50	$85	$119
	$100	$80	$112
$6,000	$25	$108	$151
	$50	$103	$144
	$100	$98	$137
$7,000	$25	$126	$177
	$50	$121	$169
	$100	$116	$162
$8,000	$25	$144	$202
	$50	$139	$195
	$100	$134	$188
$9,000	$25	$162	$227
	$50	$157	$220
	$100	$152	$213
$10,000	$25	$180	$252
	$50	$175	$245
	$100	$170	$238

Need more protection?

For amounts over $10,000, please call CSI direct at (888) 411-4911 or e-mail service@csiprotection.com

Order Student Personal Property Protector Plus℠ now!

Underwritten by Fireman's Fund Insurance Company

Sign up online at www.csiprotection.com or complete the form below.

Please see adjacent chart for premium rates.

Insurance Amount $ _____

☐ Actual Cash Value ☐ Replacement Value

Deductible Amount ☐ $25 ☐ $50 ☐ $100

Annual Premium $ _____

Plus $10.00 policy processing fee $ _____

☐ Enclosed is my check payable to
CSI Insurance Agency, Inc. $ _____

☐ Visa ☐ Am Ex ☐ Master Card ☐ Discover

ACCOUNT #: _____ EXPIRATION DATE: _____
MO. / YR.

Your policy will be sent to this address:

PLEASE PRINT

Student's Name _____

Home Address: _____

_____

Tel: ( ) _____ E-mail: _____

College or University _____

Address at College: _____

CITY _____ STATE _____ ZIP _____

Housing:

☐ On campus ☐ Off campus ☐ Commuting

Please mail this form to:

CSI Insurance Agency, Inc.
104 Bombay Lane PO Box 1207
Roswell GA 30077-1207

Tel: (888) 411-4911   FAX: (678) 832-4910
E-mail: info@csiprotection.com
www.csiprotection.com

Office Use Only: EYN-2002

Add it up!

Most students own $5,000-$10,000 in property, from the text books and cell phones in their backpacks to the TVs, computers, and stereo equipment in their homes. The cost of replacing these valuables from theft, fire, water, or smoke damage can add up quickly.

With CSI's Student Personal Property Protector Plus[SM] the only thing you'll have to worry about is grades.

Personal Property Inventory

Theft, fire, smoke, or water damage can destroy your valuables, ruining your entire school year, not just your day.

To see how quickly the value of your personal property adds up, fill out the inventory list below.

Item	$ Value
Computer	$
Stereo	$
Text books	$
Television	$
VCR	$
Musical Instruments	$
Clothes	$
Sports Equipment	$
Furniture	$
Cell phone	$
TOTAL	$

Individual Items

When requesting your policy, list individual items valued over $1,000.

Item Description	$ Value

Here is the fine print

The insurance policy itself, not this brochure, forms the contract between you and the insurance company. The policy may contain limits, exclusions, and limitations that are not detailed here. Coverages may vary by state.

Property Insured
Your policy insures all personal articles owned by you or in your direct care, custody, or control so long as you are an enrolled student or college staff member.

Territorial Limits
Your policy covers your property anywhere in the world provided any claim is brought within the United States.

Property Excluded
Your policy does not cover the following:
– Financial documents, stocks, cash, intellectual property, transportation or other tickets, bullion, paintings, statuary, art works, manuscripts, or mechanical drawings.
– Unexplained loss or mysterious disappearance.
– Automobiles, motorized vehicles of any kind including vehicle equipment.

Limits of Liability
The maximum liability for any one loss is limited to the total amount of your policy.

Other Restrictions
■ Bicycles are limited to $500 unless separately listed in the policy.
■ Items in storage are limited to $1,000 unless stored with an approved facility.
■ Jewelry, watches, precious stones or metals, fine arts, and musical instruments are limited to 20% of the limit of liability, to a maximum of $2,000.
■ Any jewelry or musical instruments valued over $1,000 must be separately listed in order to be covered.
■ Computer software, music or video CDs, DVDs or tapes will be replaced at their actual cash value at the time of loss provided original proof of purchase is provided.

Period of Coverage
Coverage shall only apply to loss occurring within the period shown in the policy.

Renewal
Renewals, subject to our underwriting policy, will be automatically renewed upon receipt of the renewal premium.

Fraud
This policy is void in case of fraud by you in obtaining the policy or if you intentionally conceal or misrepresent a material fact concerning the policy, the property covered, your interest in the covered property, or the loss circumstances.

CSI Insurance Agency, Inc.
104 Bombay Lane PO Box 1207
Roswell GA 30077-1207

Tel: (888) 411-4911
FAX: (678) 832-4910
E-mail: info@csiprotection.com
www.csiprotection.com

Fireman's Fund®

CAR INSURANCE

The Independent Insurance Agents of America report that 70% of all students who own cars now bring them to college. Whether you are a member of that 70% or not could affect your car insurance or your parents' car insurance, so give your agent a call to tell them:

- When and where you're going to college.

- Whether you're taking your car with you or leaving it at home.

Leaving The Car At Home

Many colleges do not allow freshmen to keep cars on campus. Even if you are allowed a car, you may decide you don't want to bring one. Either way, if you were on your parents' car insurance policy at home during high school, their rates will probably change when you go to school.

Even if your parents keep you on their policy when you go to school, they should still get a discount on their premiums. This is especially true if you go to a school that's more than 100 miles from home.

When you move to college your insurer assumes you won't be able to drive your car as often, so the possibility of having an accident is reduced. However, if you remain on the policy, you can still drive when you go home for breaks. One word of caution: Make sure you know what's considered a break and what is considered moving home. You may need to make another change to your policy next summer if you live at home and want to be covered.

An alternative would be for your parents to take you off their policy completely to save even more money. In this case, know under what circumstances—if any—you could still drive the car.

Bringing The Car With You

If you decide to bring a car to campus, you need to tell your insurance agent.

First, tell your agent where you are moving to make sure you'll be covered. Your current policy is based on having your car in your hometown, but when you move to college, the risk of insuring you will change. Imagine if you're currently living in Smalltown, U.S.A. with a zero crime rate and one traffic light, but will be going to school in a big city. Obviously, your chance of getting into an accident or damaging your car increases at your new school. Your insurer has the right to increase your rates to cover your increased risk. Keeping your car in a new location without telling your agent may violate your existing policy, and if something did happen, your insurance company could deny you coverage!

If you rent a car...you'll want liability insurance in case you cause an accident. If you already have car insurance, it's likely that your liability coverage will extend to the rental car, but check first. If you're not covered, you may want to consider buying liability coverage at the car rental counter!

Telling your agent about your move will also help you be sure you're covered in full, since different states have different requirements for the types and levels of insurance coverage.

When updating your insurance policy, make sure you check for any potential discounts. A few ways to save include:

Getting good grades: You may be able to save as much as 25% on your premiums if you maintain at least a B average, make the dean's list, or are in the top 20% of your class. And the great thing about being a good student is that this discount could continue even after you graduate; college students are often eligible for this discount until they are 25 or get married.

Being a good driver: A clean record with no previous accidents or moving violations (like speeding tickets) will save you big.

Driving less: If you don't drive that much, insurance companies will often give you a discount. Usually companies have certain thresholds you need to be under, such as less than 5,000 or 10,000 miles per year. As a student you may qualify.

Sticking with one company: Having your car insurance and renter's insurance from the same company may save you on both policies!

HEALTH INSURANCE

In addition to insuring your property, you'll want to insure yourself. Getting hurt or ill is stressful enough; you don't want to have to worry about how you're going to pay for your health care, too. Getting sick without health insurance can mean paying medical bills for a long time after you've recovered.

As a student, you're most likely to get your health insurance under your parents' family policy or through your college. Many schools require that you have health insurance, so if you're unable to provide proof that you are covered by your parents' policy or your own, they'll insist that you buy coverage under their plan.

Staying On Your Family Plan

Many insurance companies allow children who are full-time students to remain on their parents' plan until they are 26. If this is the case, and you have the option of remaining on your parents' plan, it's probably the least expensive way to keep health insurance. Make sure you understand your coverage before you leave for campus. Most insurance companies have a toll-free number you can call with questions. Be sure to ask:

Which doctors you can go to: Depending on your parents' plan, your choice of doctors near your school may be limited. Ask how to find a doctor in your area.

What is covered: You should know what your plan covers. Does it cover preventative care like an annual physical? Some schools will require a physical and booster shots before you move to campus. Does it only cover emergency care? What about psychological care or counseling? Ask ahead of time, before you're in trouble.

What you are responsible for paying: Most insurance companies will require you to share in the cost of your healthcare by making co-payments for office visits and prescriptions. Find out how much these are.

What to do in case of an emergency: Some insurance companies require that you call a toll-free number, while others ask you to call your primary doctor before you go to the emergency room. Make sure you know what to do, since these charges tend to rack up faster than cars at the Daytona 500.

COBRA Coverage

If you aren't going to school full-time or can't continue on your family's policy for any reason, you may be able to get around the problem by using COBRA coverage. COBRA, short for the Consolidated Omnibus Budget Reconciliation Act, may allow you to keep your coverage for up to 18 months, as long as you pay the premium. This could be expensive, however, so you should see if you qualify for a less expensive college plan.

Getting On Your College Plan

A very popular option for students is to get health insurance through a plan offered by their college. Generally this type of coverage runs less than $1,000 per year, more affordable than getting it on your own. Since benefits vary greatly depending on your school's plan, read your policy carefully, keeping an eye out for information that answers the same questions you asked about staying on your family's policy: what is covered, which doctors you can go to, what you must pay, and what to do in case of emergency. Also know that some plans may not cover you over the summer.

Health Services

In addition to offering you access to health insurance, your college may also have its own set of doctors and care facilities on campus, generally called Health Services. As a student you may be required to pay an additional fee for this service as part of your tuition, but it tends to be very convenient when dealing with minor ailments. Health Services generally offers office hours for you to get physicals, X-rays, counseling services, or emergency care. There's usually a pharmacy to fill your prescriptions, too.

CHAPTER TEN

FINANCING YOUR EDUCATION

Y ou've figured out what you need for college, from what to pack to where to buy a computer and what bank account you need. But none of that will matter if you can't pay your tuition.

By the time you're packing up and preparing to leave for campus, you've most likely completed the majority of your financial planning through your college's financial aid office. But there are sources of aid outside your college too. This chapter will teach you about additional options for finding and using scholarships, loans, and military service to help pay for college.

SCHOLARSHIPS

You don't need to be an academic genius or athletic super-star to get a scholarship; nor is your school the only way you can get one. Scholarships are available for students interested in particular fields of study or those who come from certain ethnic backgrounds or geographic areas. You can even find scholarships for students with specific birth dates!

Where To Look

One of the best places to scholarship-hunt is the Internet. When you go online you can create a personalized search based on your background and interests. It's also fast, and sometimes even free. The website you're using will take the information you enter and match it with a database of scholarships to give you information on applying to those for which you qualify.

There are numerous online databases that combine infor-mation on scholarships and other types of financial aid programs from national, state, public, and private sources. Checking out each of the databases is a great idea. Even though some of the information overlaps, each database also has information that the others don't. You've got to look around. This might be "free" money, but you've still got to work for it!

You should also check with the financial aid office at your new school and with guidance counselors at your high school. And if you really want to leave no stone unturned, check the bulletin boards at your local library and colleges.

Avoiding Scams

When searching for scholarships, be sure to avoid scams—there are a lot of them out there. Every year hundreds of thousands of students and their parents are victims of fraudulent companies claiming to help them get "free" money for college.

To avoid being a victim yourself, be wary of the following details that have indicated scams in the past:

- Anyone who asks you to send money to apply for a scholarship.

- Any time you are notified that you have won a scholarship, but that you must pay a redemption or disbursement fee, or taxes on your winnings, before they can send you the check.

- Any promises of money-back guarantees for which the refunds will be almost impossible to get.

- Free financial-aid seminars that lure you in with the promise of advice and then pressure you to purchase insurance, annuity, and investment products. Don't be afraid to walk out!

Even though scams exist, that doesn't mean every scholarship service that charges a fee is a bad idea. Some firms will require a fee in exchange for providing services above and beyond those that you can get for free. Certainly, if these services help you find a scholarship that the free services do not, they're worth every penny. Just be sure you know what you're getting for your money.

LOANS AND PAYMENT PLANS

Scholarships may be "free" money, but with loans, you have to pay the money back—in most cases plus interest. Because of this, loans are usually easier to get than scholarships, and your parents can get them too. Loans come in four major categories:

Scholarship Experts

Loans For Students

According to FinAid.org, the average college student graduates with $16,500 in loans.

Typically, students will be awarded loans as part of their financial aid package after they have completed the Free Application for Federal Student Aid (FAFSA) form. Through this process, students can be awarded either Federal Stafford Loans or Federal Perkins Loans.

Stafford loans: These are the most common loans. They are awarded on a subsidized or unsubsidized basis. Subsidized Stafford Loans are awarded when the student demonstrates financial need. The government pays the interest on the loan while the student is in school. Alternatively, with an unsubsidized loan, the student is  responsible for the interest immediately, although payment can often be deferred until after graduation. Many students take out a combination of subsidized and unsubsidized Stafford loans to pay for school, but the federal government limits the total amount that can be borrowed on Stafford Loans. Although these amounts are subject to change, students are currently allowed to borrow $2,625 for freshman year, $3,500 for sophomore year, and $5,500 for each of junior and senior years. Students who are financially independent are allowed to borrow additional amounts.

Perkins loans: Students love to see that they've been awarded a Perkins Loan since they're all subsidized (students don't pay for the interest while they're in school) and are subject to the lowest interest rates. Only the most

financially-needy students will receive these loans; the federal government limits the amount each college can award, so there's less money to go around. If you're awarded a Perkins Loan, your college financial aid office will determine how much you receive up to the limit set by the federal government: $3,000 per year.

Loans For Parents

There are also federally funded loans for parents: the Parent Loan for Undergraduate Students (PLUS). With a PLUS loan parents can borrow up to the entire cost of the student's tuition, books, supplies, and even living expenses, minus whatever the family receives in student aid. The interest rates on these loans will vary each year, but will never exceed 9%. To qualify for a PLUS loan, parents must be U.S. citizens and have good credit history, but there are no income or collateral requirements.

In addition to PLUS loans, parents also have a variety of other options. One very popular choice for parents who own their own home is to take out a home equity loan or a home equity line of credit. One reason many parents prefer the line of credit over the loan is that they can borrow money and pay interest on it only as needed, rather than deciding how much to borrow and paying interest from the beginning. Therefore, if your parents' circumstances change for the better or worse, they can borrow accordingly. Of course, before making any decisions it's a good idea to compare the interest rates being charged on the PLUS loans with those on the potential home equity loan or line of credit.

Private Loans

If you still can't make ends meet after borrowing under the federally-funded loan programs, or if you are looking for different repayment options, private loans may be the answer. These loans, also known as alternative loans, are funded by private lenders like banks, so there are no federal forms to fill out. Parents may want to borrow from private lenders because they allow them to delay repayment until after the student graduates, something the federal loans do not allow. To learn more about private loans, check online or with your local financial institutions.

Payment Plans

For parents who can't swing paying their portion of a year or semester's worth of tuition up front, payment plans can be a good choice, either in addition to or instead of a loan. Offered at most universities, these plans allow parents to spread out their contribution over 10 to 12 monthly payments rather than having to pay in one lump sum. The payment plan at your college will usually be administered by one of a few major companies offering these plans, or by the school itself. Most plans don't charge interest, but instead, you'll be expected to pay a small enrollment fee, normally around $40 or $50, and possibly a finance charge. For more information about the payment plans your school accepts and the fees they charge, check with your financial aid office.

MILITARY SERVICE

If you're inspired to both go to college and serve your country, enlisting in the military may be a good way to finance your education. When investigating this opportunity, you should consult the website belonging to the branch of the military you are interested in joining: The Army (www.goarmy.com), Navy (www.navy.com), Marines (www.marines.com), Air Force (www.airforce.com), or Coast Guard (www.uscg.mil). Then speak with your local recruiter.

Joining the military can be a great experience and a good way to pay for a large portion of your college education. However, it is also a long-term commitment that will not only affect your life during college, but also your life after college. Get all the facts, and when considering this option keep in mind:

Each Branch Is Different

Afraid of heights? Can't swim? When considering which branch of the service might be right for you, think about who you are and what you find interesting (or frightening). Furthermore, consider this in combination with the financial aid programs that each branch offers. Many financial aid programs are offered by multiple branches of the service, while others are unique to one or two. If you decide to enlist, your decision regarding which branch you serve should be a combination of personal interests and financial considerations.

Money Vs. Commitment

Perhaps the most important consideration is the tradeoff between how much money you need and how much time you are willing to commit. Options vary from serving on a full-time basis to being a reservist only required to serve two weeks per year and one weekend per month. You can also choose to begin your service before, during, or after college. Based on that decision, your financial aid will vary from receiving money during college in terms of a scholarship, salary, or stipend to not receiving money until after graduation. You would then use that money to pay off loans you took out during school.

The last thing you should ask yourself is whether or not you would be prepared to serve if called. Joining the military is a big commitment, and could even result in active wartime duty. That said, it's an opportunity that provides unparalleled experience and is a great resume builder. Just make sure it's the right choice for you before enrolling.

CHAPTER ELEVEN

GETTING
A JOB

Considering how much college costs, it's not surprising that many students contemplate getting jobs. In fact, over half of all students end up working during the school year.

If you find yourself pondering student employment, you can take comfort in a recent study by Sebago Associates that shows working part-time won't necessarily bring down your grades. On the contrary, they found that working part-time often provided valuable experience and developed time-management skills that helped students do better in school.

In deciding what's right for you, remember that only you know your financial situation and personal limits. Without a doubt, working can mean less time for studying, socializing, and sleeping, so consider your situation carefully. This chapter will help you decide how much you should work during school (if at all) and how to find a suitable job on or off campus.

HOW MUCH SHOULD YOU WORK?

Before you decide whether or not to look for a job it's important to ask yourself why you'll be working and how much time you can realistically spend at a job.

If you decide that you're simply choosing to work to earn extra spending money or to start building your resume, you might want to consider waiting until at least your second semester. This will give you a grace period to figure out how much time you need to attend classes, study, and participate in activities. Otherwise, if you're working in order to pay your bills, decide how much money you need and how much time you can spare. With luck, you can find a job that meets both these criteria.

According to Student Monitor, 60% of all students work during the school year and 85% work during the summer. On average, students earn $4,860 per year.

Students working out of financial necessity may have something called "work-study" as part of their financial aid packages. Work-study is funded by the federal government and awarded by the College Scholarship Board when you apply for financial aid. Receiving a work-study award means that the college expects you to pay for some portion of your expenses through employment. The size of your work-study award will basically tell you how much you're expected to work. For instance, if you were given a work-study for $1,000 per semester, assuming that most student jobs pay $8 per hour and most semesters are 15 weeks in length, then you are expected to work roughly 8 hours per week ($1,000 per semester / $8 per hour / 15 weeks per semester). Of course, if you want to, you can also usually choose to work more.

Don't worry if your first job at school is less glamorous than you were hoping. Many students find ordinary jobs like reshelving library books or cleaning tables in the dining hall a nice break from the stresses of college life. You'll have plenty of time to build your resume after settling in, or even better—during your summer breaks!

Most jobs will require a commitment of at least 5 to 10 hours per week. If you are unsure if you can commit that much, you may want to consider jobs in which you work only when you choose, such as participating in psychology experiments, babysitting, or working as a temporary employee ("temping") for an area business. If you choose to work more than the minimum, it's recommended that you limit yourself to 10 to 20 hours per week. Most educators agree that grades do suffer when students work more than that. This is especially true for students working more than 35 hours per week, who are much more likely to drop out of school than those working fewer hours.

FINDING THE RIGHT JOB FOR YOU

Once you've decided to work, it's nice to know that most jobs at college are extremely flexible. It's your job to decide when you want to work and what type of environment you find most appealing. Do you want somewhere quiet, like the library, or bustling, like the dining hall? Would you prefer to work alone, performing research or cleaning lab equipment, or do you like the interaction of leading campus tours or waiting tables in a nearby restaurant? College

students can work in a wide variety of jobs depending on their interests, but some of the more common ones include:

- Library aide

- Office assistant

- Computer technical support

- Tutor

- Researcher

- Lab assistant

- Ticket agent or usher

- Copy center assistant

When thinking about which job is best for you, realize that in most cases there's a trade-off between how much you're paid and what kind of work you're doing. If simply making money to pay your bills is your top priority, then you should probably just pick the best-paying job (within reason, of course—we all have our limits!). But if you have some flexibility in how much you need to make or how much time you can spend, think about a job that pays a little less per hour, but offers opportunities to learn new skills, make contacts, and build your resume. These jobs could include anything from research positions with professors to work in a key college administrative office, such as financial aid.

You should also decide whether you want to work on or off campus. Typically, jobs that are on campus are more flexible and understanding of student schedules. During exam periods you will likely be able to find other students with whom to trade shifts, and because the jobs also tend to coincide with the school calendar, you usually won't be expected to work during break. And jobs on campus are a great way to meet fellow students.

On the other hand, for some students, off-campus jobs are a better choice. Depending on where your college is located, there will be different opportunities available, but in general, jobs off campus allow you to interact with people outside the college community and often open doors to larger opportunities such as summer internships. One word of caution: When evaluating off-campus jobs, make sure transportation won't be a problem. Getting to your job must be quick and convenient. Time spent commuting is still time away from your studies, but you're not getting paid for it!

MAID IT!

I found my first part-time job in college on the student employment office's website. What caught my eye was the pay rate: $25/hour, with a flexible schedule. The only problem was the actual work I would have to do; I would essentially be a maid for a middle-aged man who lived near campus: washing dishes, vacuuming, and doing the laundry. But even if the work wasn't exactly up my alley, I figured for that much money it was worth a shot.

At first, everything went fine. My new boss gave me a tour of his apartment, showed me his vacuum cleaner, briefed me on his laundry ("Never, never put this sweater in the dryer!"), and we set up a once-a-week schedule. For the first couple of weeks, I showed up, did two hours of work, and collected $50. It was far from easy, though; each week he left me a huge hamper full of sweaty clothes and a week's worth of dirty dishes in the sink.

In my third week, I found my employer waiting for me with a sour look on his face. In the kitchen he showed me grease and melted-on cheese gunk I had failed to scrub off of his favorite frying pan the previous week. I didn't bother to explain the difficulty of removing six-day-old cheese from metal, but politely agreed to try harder. That week I scrubbed the pots with all my strength, but in between running back and forth to the laundry room and untangling the cord of the vacuum cleaner, I knew there were a couple of dishes that still weren't exactly spotless.

In my fourth week, I was fired. My boss wasn't cruel about it, and I wasn't too disappointed—I wasn't planning a career in domestic services anyway.

A few weeks later, a couple of my friends heard about another job they thought I might like. It paid slightly less per hour, but because it was much better suited to my personal skills, I enjoyed my work a lot more and I stayed with it for a couple of years.

- Jon D., Harvard University

Once you've narrowed down your choices, you need to know how to find interesting job openings. While there are many jobs that need to be filled, there's still a lot of competition for the most desirable ones. If you have your heart set on working in the library or in a certain office, it might pay for you to get to campus a few days early so you can apply before most of your competition arrives.

If you're not fortunate enough to land that dream job, or if you're not sure exactly what you want to do, there are many ways of learning about job openings on or off campus. The first stop for most students is the student employment office. Here you should find all the listings for openings on campus and get help writing any cover letters or resumes you may need. The student employment offices at most schools have websites you can search for jobs by location, area of interest, and desired hours per week, right from your dorm room!

When deciding on a job, don't forget to consider perks, also known as fringe benefits. For instance, if you work in a dining hall or restaurant, you may get free food. If you work in the athletics or theater department, you might get tickets to see events for free. For those who love to shop, consider working at one of your favorite stores to earn an employee discount. Over the long haul, these savings can really add up!

While you're online, you should also check out the various websites that cater to students looking for part-time jobs. These sites will connect you with employers in various industries that have a lot of part-time positions, such as retail, entertainment, and food service. They also let you know who's hiring.

For those of you who prefer the old-fashioned route, be sure to buy copies of the campus and local newspapers and check out their Help Wanted sections. Talk to as many people as possible to learn about jobs that may not have been advertised, and take a walk around town to spot help-wanted signs posted in windows.

CONGRATULATIONS!

That's it! You're one step closer to being a successful college freshman.

As anyone who's gone to college knows, getting ready for your first year is a big deal, with lots of changes and decisions to make. Fortunately, you've given yourself a head start by reading this guide. You've learned some of the most important information about preparing for college life:

What to bring: When packing for school, less is more. You won't need that third umbrella or those two hundred CDs to enjoy life on campus. Cover your bases by calling roommates and your college first; you don't want two TVs or two microwaves and you certainly don't want any halogen lamps if your school doesn't allow them. The dorm is the ultimate communal area: Don't bring anything with you that you don't want to share or can't afford to lose. You'll probably want a computer, so start thinking desktop or laptop—and don't forget to phone home, whether from a regular or cell phone.

How to get it there: This is one of the biggest trips of your life. But you're not worried about moving all that stuff, because you won't overpack, you'll get the right kind of help with your move, and you've planned a restful stop at the Grand Canyon on the way. Even though your airline may not be publicizing a student discount, you'll remember to ask if there is one and consult your travel agent.

How to pay for it: Going to college is as much a financial education as an academic one. Look for a bank account with low fees you understand. Consider getting your first credit card and if you do, use it responsibly (pay your bill and don't spend more than you can afford). And check with an insurance agent to make sure you and your belongings are covered in case anything unfortunate happens. Think about getting a job, and what kind of job you can handle.

Now you're ready to go about the business of moving to college, but remember: This book will be here for you when you have a question ("What is it that I'm supposed to look for in a credit card?") or when you want to reminisce about the days before you were an expert. Until then...

Go. Have fun! Make the most of college.

Tell Us What You Think For A Chance To Win $500!

You're going to college, so you could probably use an extra $500 for tuition, books, clothes, or to spruce up your new dorm room....and you could win just by telling us what you think of this book!

Your opinion is important to us—we want to know your take so that we can improve *Everything You Need For College* for future students. Did you find it helpful? What did you like? What could have been better? Your views will help those going to college in years to come. And you could end up with a nice chunk of extra cash!

Complete our brief survey online at www.eynfc.com/survey and you'll be automatically entered to win. We'll randomly select one lucky respondent to get the cash! It could be you!

For your chance to win, go now to:

www.eynfc.com/survey

For complete information and rules, see the next page or visit our rules online at: **www.eynfc.com/survey/rules**

SWEEPSTAKES RULES

1. **Eligibility**: Open to U.S. Residents. Entrants must be high school seniors or older. VOID WHERE PROHIBITED BY LAW. Employees or agents of EYN Media, Inc., and members of their immediate families (defined as spouse, children, parents, or siblings) or households are NOT eligible to enter.

2. **How to enter:** NO PURCHASE NECESSARY. The sweepstakes runs from May 1, 2002 through August 30, 2002. There are two ways to enter. Online: Entrants may enter online by following instructions at www.eynfc.com/survey. Required fields will be marked by an asterisk. By Postal Mail: Print your (i) name, (ii) complete address, (iii) phone number, (iv) date of birth, (v) college, and (vi) how you received *Everything You Need For College* on a postcard and mail it to EYN Media, Inc., 12 Arrow Street, Suite 303, Cambridge, MA 02138. Limit one entry per person, regardless of entry method. Duplicate entries will be voided. All online entries must be received by 5 p.m. EDT on August 30, 2002. All postal mail entries must be postmarked by August 15, 2002.

3. **Prize:** EYN Media, Inc. will award $500 to the winner of the sweepstakes.

4. **Selection of winner and odds of winning:** Winner will be selected by random drawing by EYN Media, Inc. The drawing will take place on September 16, 2002. All decisions made by EYN Media, Inc. are final. Odds of winning depend on number of qualified entries received. Prize may not be substituted or transferred. Winner will be notified by e-mail (if entry was completed online) or mail and phone (if entry was completed by mail) within fourteen days after the drawing. Alternate winner will be selected at random for an unclaimed prize after the fourteenth day following the first attempted notification. All taxes are the sole responsibility of the prize winner.

5. **Privacy policy:** Entrant's responses to the survey will be used solely for the purposes of (i) improving subsequent editions of the guidebook and (ii) compiling aggregate, anonymous consumer and demographic information. EYN Media, Inc. will not share, trade or sell identifiable individual information with any outside organization. To view EYN Media, Inc.'s privacy policy, go to www.eynfc.com/privacy. However, all entrants acknowledge that EYN is required to make certain individual information available, pursuant to Section 8 of these rules, to those who contact EYN Media, Inc. after October 15, 2002 seeking to learn who won the sweepstakes.

6. **Conditions and limitations of liability:** Sweepstakes entrants agree to abide by these official rules and the decisions of EYN Media, Inc. Decisions made by EYN Media, Inc. are final and binding on all matters pertaining to this sweepstakes. All entries are deemed to be made by the person whose name and address appears in the entry form. EYN Media, Inc. assumes no liability for problems connected with the Internet portion of the survey, including incorrect, inaccurate, or partial capture of data entry due to technical malfunctions of telephone networks or lines, servers, network problems, computer systems, human error, defective computer equipment, or traffic congestion on the Internet. EYN Media, Inc. reserves the right to cancel or suspend the sweepstakes if virus, bugs, or other causes beyond EYN Media, Inc.'s control corrupt or impede administration, security, or proper play of the sweepstakes. EYN Media, Inc., its employees and agents assume no responsibility for incomplete or incorrect submissions or misdirected or undeliverable mail sent through the U.S. Postal Service.

7. **Indemnification and release:** EYN Media, Inc. reserves the right to use the winner's name and likeness in advertising without additional compensation. Winner will be asked to sign a release allowing the use of his or her name and likeness for promotional purposes as a condition of receiving the prize. By entering the sweepstakes, participants and winners release EYN Media, Inc. from any liability arising from participation in this sweepstakes or from the acceptance, possession, use, or misuse of the prize.

8. **Winner's name:** The prize winner's name will be available after October 15, 2002. To receive this name, send a self-addressed, stamped envelope to EYN Media, Inc., 12 Arrow Street, Suite 303, Cambridge, MA 02138, with a note indicating that you would like to know who won the sweepstakes.

9. **Company contact information:**

   EYN Media, Inc.
   12 Arrow Street
   Suite 303
   Cambridge, MA 02138
   617-234-7380
   sweepstakes@eynmedia.com

INDEX OF FEATURED ADVERTISERS

Please support our sponsors!